BART SIMPSON™
BUST-UP

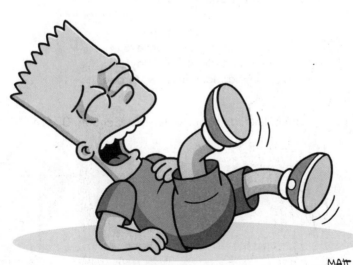

HARPER
DESIGN
An Imprint of HarperCollinsPublishers

BART SIMPSON BUST-UP

Bart Simpson #73, #74, #75, #76, #77, and Summer Shindig #7

Copyright © 2018 by
Bongo Entertainment, Inc. All rights reserved.
No part of this book may be used or reproduced in any manner whatsoever
without written permission except in the case of brief quotations
embodied in critical articles and reviews. For information address
HarperCollins Publishers,
195 Broadway, New York, New York 10007.

FIRST EDITION

ISBN 978-0-06-269255-9
Library of Congress Control Number 2017936290
18 19 20 21 22 TC 10 9 8 7 6 5 4 3 2 1

Publisher: Matt Groening

Creative Director: Nathan Kane
Managing Editor: Terry Delegeane
Director of Operations: Robert Zaugh
Art Director: Jason Ho
Production Manager: Christopher Ungar
Assistant Editor: Karen Bates
Production: Art Villanueva
Administration: Ruth Waytz
Legal Guardian: Susan A. Grode

Printed by TC Transcontinental, Beauceville, QC, Canada. 02/14/2018

BART SIMPSON™
MATT GROENING

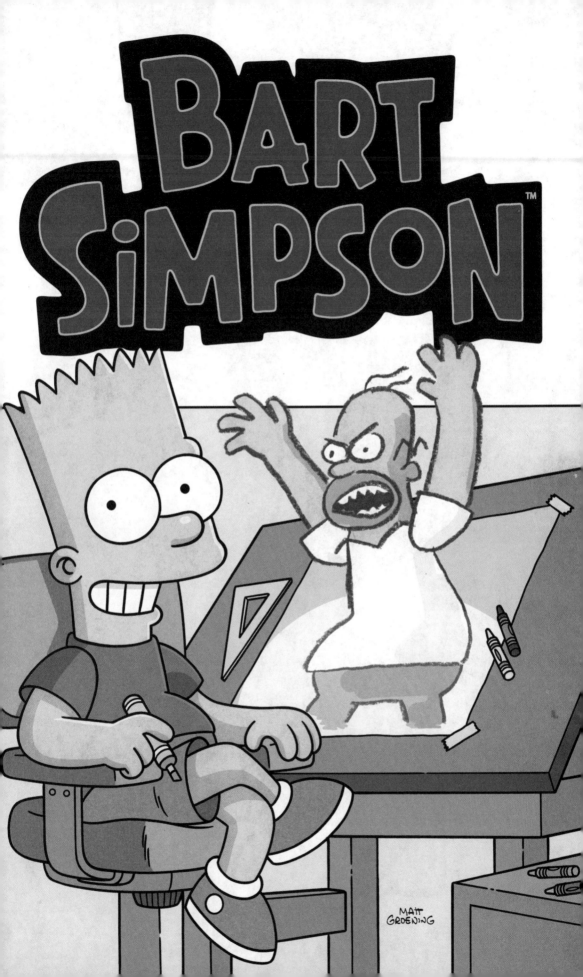

MATT GROENING

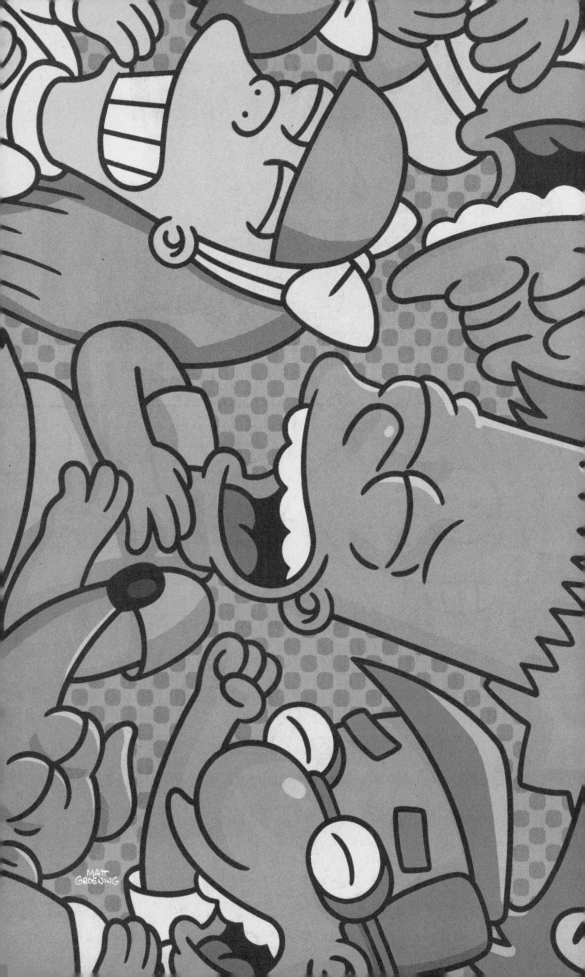

SOON...
I'VE GOT TO HAND IT TO YOU, BART. YOU DID THE RIGHT THING! COMING BACK HERE TO THE COACH SECTION WASN'T SO BAD, WAS IT?
I'M SURPRISED! BUT SOMETIMES YOU CAN DO THE RIGHT THING...

"...AND STILL PUT ONE OVER ON MARTIN!"
PLEASE! EVERYONE! USE THE BATHROOM ***ONE AT A TIME!***
ROOM SERVICE! ROOM SERVICE! ***SEND UP A LARGER ROOM!***
YOU STOLE THAT FROM ***GROUCHO MARX,*** DUDE.
THE END

STRANGE. EVERYONE IN COACH USUALLY GOES FOR A WALK DURING THESE STATION STOPS. GUESS THEY REALLY LIKE IT INSIDE.
FIRST CLASS
WHO ARE THESE PEOPLE?
JUST A FEW FRIENDS OF MINE. TOLD YOU THERE'S ROOM HERE, GUYS!
TEN BUCKS, PLEASE!
DON'T WORRY. I ONLY MADE THE OFFER TO THE PEOPLE WHO WERE SITTING NEXT TO US.
BUT EVERY-ONE WAS SITTING NEXT TO US!
BART! YOU'VE GOT TO DO SOME-THING!
I KNOW, I KNOW.
MUCH AS I HATE TO DO IT, I'VE GOT TO FIND MARTIN AND TELL HIM I WANT TO TRADE BACK!
CHARLIE

SORRY...MY SISTER GETS A LITTLE LOST SOMETIMES. HER TICKET'S BACK IN OUR ROOM. WE'LL BE DINING IN, OKAY?
FIRST CLASS
CERTAINLY, SIR.
THIS IS THE MEAL MY STOMACH'S BEEN WAITING FOR ALL ITS LIFE. SEEMS A *CRIME* NOT TO SHARE IT!
:GROAN!: I *KNEW* YOU WERE GOING TO SAY THAT.
SEE, THERE'S AN ERROR ON THE TICKET. I'M NOT MARTIN PRINCE...I'M *PRINCE MARTIN*. THIS IS MY LADY-IN-WAITING!
WHAT A HORRIBLE MISTAKE, SIR. OF COURSE THEY CAN GO AHEAD!
OH, THIS IS HEAVENLY! BUT I MISS YOUR FATHER.
RIGHT, RIGHT! I'M ON IT.
I'M PROUD OF YOU, BART. IT'S LIKE THE *UNDERGROUND RAILROAD*!
IT LOOKED PRETTY *ABOVE GROUND* TO ME!
YOU KNOW, BOY, THERE'S NO REASON WE SHOULD LET A GOOD THING LIKE THIS GO TO WASTE.
HOO-BOY...

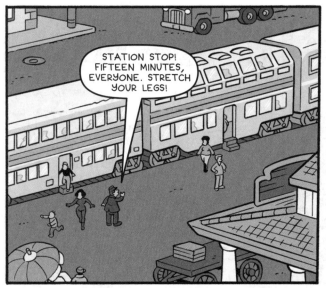

STATION STOP! FIFTEEN MINUTES, EVERYONE. STRETCH YOUR LEGS!

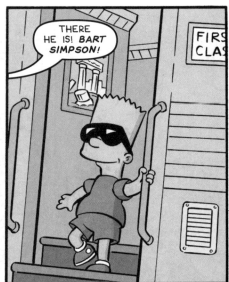

THERE HE IS! *BART SIMPSON!*

FIRST CLAS

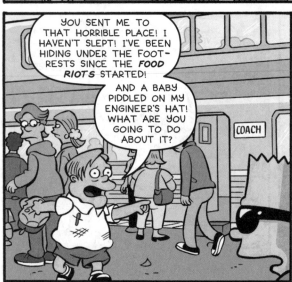

YOU SENT ME TO THAT HORRIBLE PLACE! I HAVEN'T SLEPT! I'VE BEEN HIDING UNDER THE FOOT-RESTS SINCE THE *FOOD RIOTS* STARTED!

AND A BABY PIDDLED ON MY ENGINEER'S HAT! WHAT ARE YOU GOING TO DO ABOUT IT?

COACH

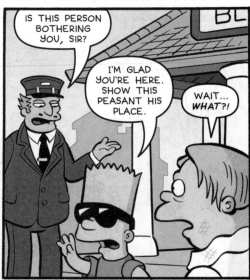

IS THIS PERSON BOTHERING YOU, SIR?

I'M GLAD YOU'RE HERE. SHOW THIS PEASANT HIS PLACE.

WAIT... *WHAT?!*

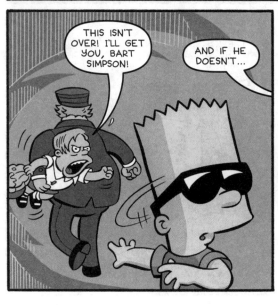

THIS ISN'T OVER! I'LL GET YOU, BART SIMPSON!

AND IF HE DOESN'T...

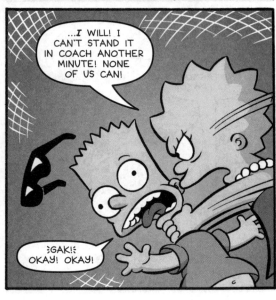

...*I* WILL! I CAN'T STAND IT IN COACH ANOTHER MINUTE! NONE OF US CAN!

≶GAK!≶ OKAY! OKAY!

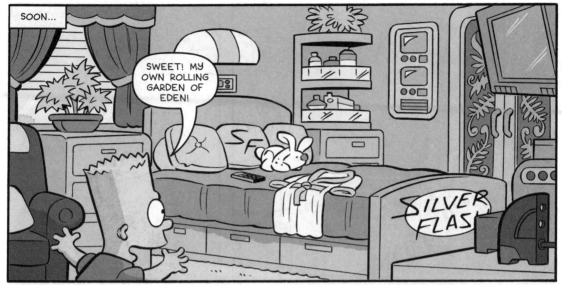

SOON...

SWEET! MY OWN ROLLING GARDEN OF EDEN!

SILVER FLAS

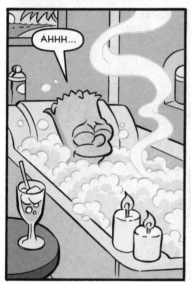

AHHH...

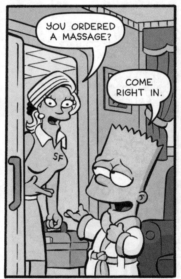

YOU ORDERED A MASSAGE?

COME RIGHT IN.

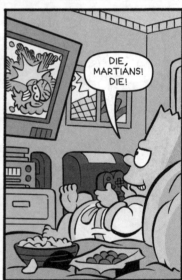

DIE, MARTIANS! DIE!

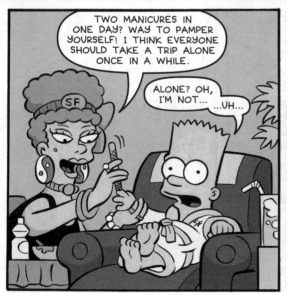

TWO MANICURES IN ONE DAY? WAY TO PAMPER YOURSELF! I THINK EVERYONE SHOULD TAKE A TRIP ALONE ONCE IN A WHILE.

ALONE? OH, I'M NOT... ...UH...

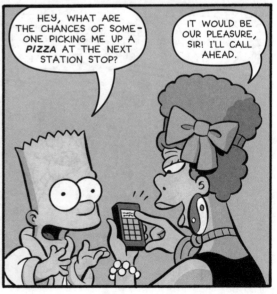

HEY, WHAT ARE THE CHANCES OF SOME-ONE PICKING ME UP A *PIZZA* AT THE NEXT STATION STOP?

IT WOULD BE OUR PLEASURE, SIR! I'LL CALL AHEAD.

MERCI BEAUCOUP, GARÇON. C'EST MAGNIFIQUE!
MERCI, MONSIEUR!
ET EEZ OUR PLEASURE TO SERVE YOU!
HE'S ABOUT TO GET SERVED ALL RIGHT!
FIRST CLASS
I'M READY TO GO BACK TO MY ROOM, MY GOOD MAN...IN FIRST CLASS.
VERY GOOD, SIR.
FIRST CLASS
AH, YOU MUST BE NEW ON SHIFT. I'M READY TO GO BACK TO MY ROOM AS WELL.
MAY I SEE YOUR TICKET?
I...I CAN'T FIND IT!
HOW UNFORTUNATE...
...FOR YOU! GET BACK IN COACH, WHERE YOU BELONG!
NO! DON'T SEND ME BACK THERE WITH THE...
...THE PEOPLE!
NO! NO!
FIRST CLASS
ENJOY THE RIDE, MARTIN. I SURE WILL!

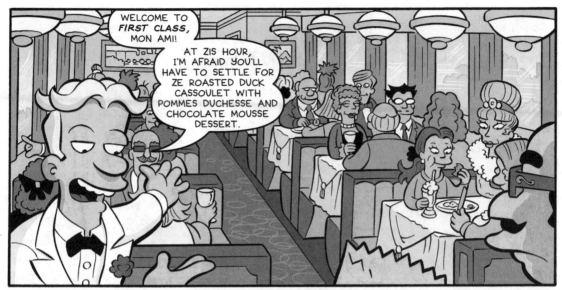

WELCOME TO *FIRST CLASS,* MON AMI!

AT ZIS HOUR, I'M AFRAID YOU'LL HAVE TO SETTLE FOR ZE ROASTED DUCK CASSOULET WITH POMMES DUCHESSE AND CHOCOLATE MOUSSE DESSERT.

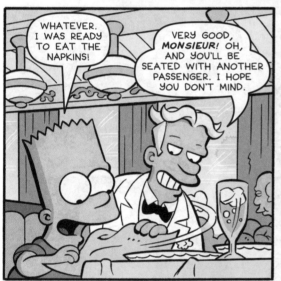

WHATEVER. I WAS READY TO EAT THE NAPKINS!

VERY GOOD, *MONSIEUR!* OH, AND YOU'LL BE SEATED WITH ANOTHER PASSENGER. I HOPE YOU DON'T MIND.

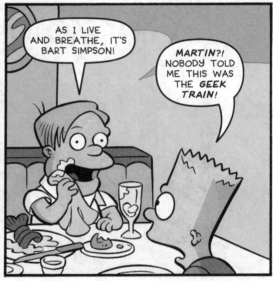

AS I LIVE AND BREATHE, IT'S BART SIMPSON!

MARTIN?! NOBODY TOLD ME THIS WAS THE *GEEK TRAIN!*

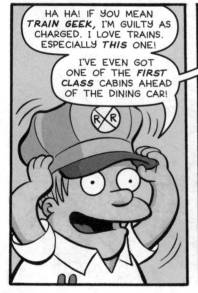

HA HA! IF YOU MEAN *TRAIN GEEK,* I'M GUILTY AS CHARGED. I LOVE TRAINS. ESPECIALLY *THIS* ONE!

I'VE EVEN GOT ONE OF THE *FIRST CLASS* CABINS AHEAD OF THE DINING CAR!

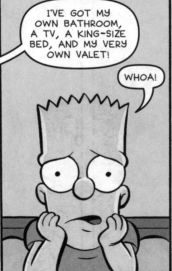

I'VE GOT MY OWN BATHROOM, A TV, A KING-SIZE BED, AND MY VERY OWN VALET!

WHOA!

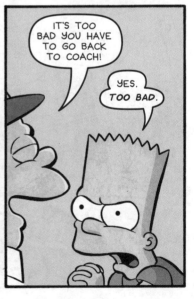

IT'S TOO BAD YOU HAVE TO GO BACK TO COACH!

YES. *TOO BAD.*

⁝SIGH!⁝ ALL MY ROMANTIC NOTIONS OF TRAIN TRAVEL ARE GONE. THEY SHOULD'VE CALLED THIS THE ***DISORIENT EXPRESS***!
TRAVEL
FACE IT, LIS. THIS IS ANOTHER ONE OF DAD'S BRILLIANT IDEAS GONE HORRIBLY--
ATTENTION, PLEASE. WE HAVE ONE MORE SEAT IN THE DINING CAR FOR OUR LAST SERVING OF THE NIGHT. MUCH AS IT PAINS ME...
...I NOW OFFER IT TO ***YOU PEOPLE*** IN COACH. ONE SEAT ONLY. WHICH ONE OF YOU WILL IT BE?
1
EMMIE
FOOOOOOD!
1
ME! ME! TAKE ME!
VERY WELL. COME WITH ME IF YOU WANT TO LIVE!
GO! LIVE WELL, SON! WE'LL REMEMBER YOU. BUT IF YOU EVER COME BACK...
...***BRING SALAD DRESSING PACKETS***!

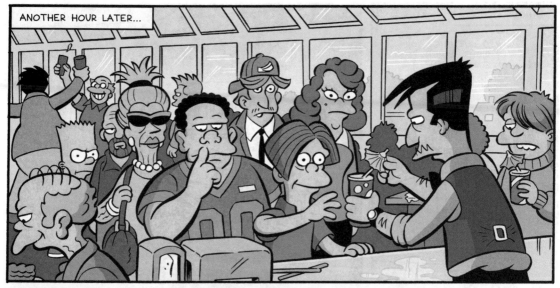

ANOTHER HOUR LATER...

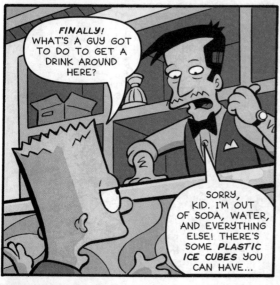

FINALLY! WHAT'S A GUY GOT TO DO TO GET A DRINK AROUND HERE?

SORRY, KID. I'M OUT OF SODA, WATER, AND EVERYTHING ELSE! THERE'S SOME *PLASTIC ICE CUBES* YOU CAN HAVE...

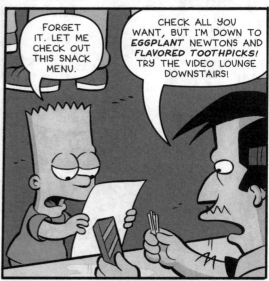

FORGET IT. LET ME CHECK OUT THIS SNACK MENU.

CHECK ALL YOU WANT, BUT I'M DOWN TO *EGGPLANT* NEWTONS AND *FLAVORED TOOTHPICKS!* TRY THE VIDEO LOUNGE DOWNSTAIRS!

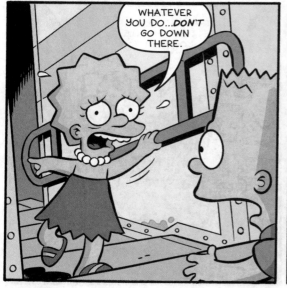

WHATEVER YOU DO...*DON'T* GO DOWN THERE.

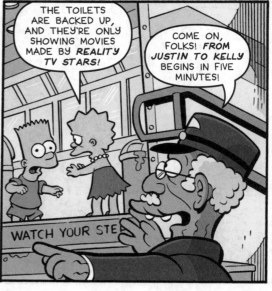

THE TOILETS ARE BACKED UP, AND THEY'RE ONLY SHOWING MOVIES MADE BY *REALITY TV STARS!*

COME ON, FOLKS! *FROM JUSTIN TO KELLY* BEGINS IN FIVE MINUTES!

WATCH YOUR STE

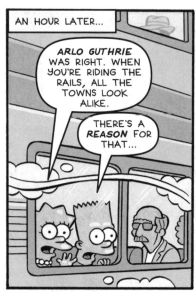

AN HOUR LATER...

ARLO GUTHRIE WAS RIGHT. WHEN YOU'RE RIDING THE RAILS, ALL THE TOWNS LOOK ALIKE.

THERE'S A *REASON* FOR THAT...

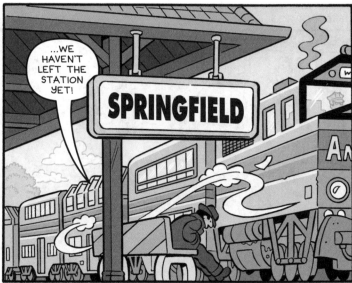

...WE HAVEN'T LEFT THE STATION YET!

SPRINGFIELD

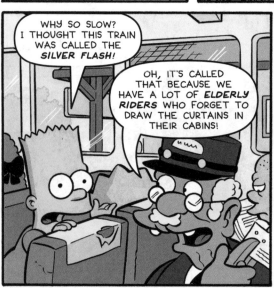

WHY SO SLOW? I THOUGHT THIS TRAIN WAS CALLED THE *SILVER FLASH!*

OH, IT'S CALLED THAT BECAUSE WE HAVE A LOT OF *ELDERLY RIDERS* WHO FORGET TO DRAW THE CURTAINS IN THEIR CABINS!

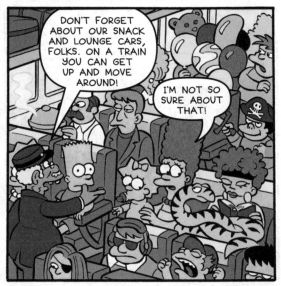

DON'T FORGET ABOUT OUR SNACK AND LOUNGE CARS, FOLKS. ON A TRAIN YOU CAN GET UP AND MOVE AROUND!

I'M NOT SO SURE ABOUT THAT!

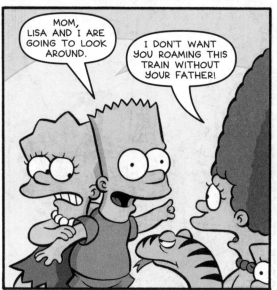

MOM, LISA AND I ARE GOING TO LOOK AROUND.

I DON'T WANT YOU ROAMING THIS TRAIN WITHOUT YOUR FATHER!

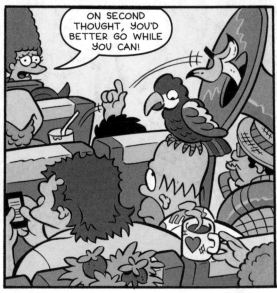

ON SECOND THOUGHT, YOU'D BETTER GO WHILE YOU CAN!

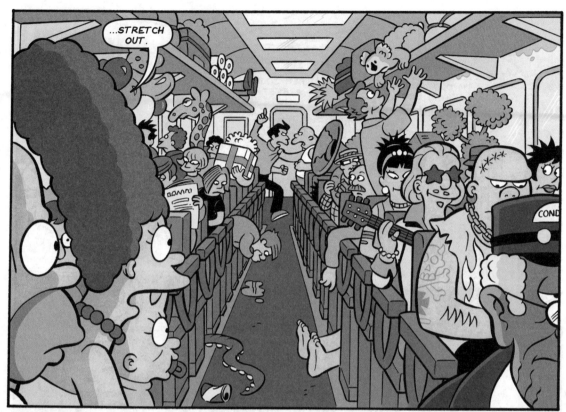

...STRETCH OUT.

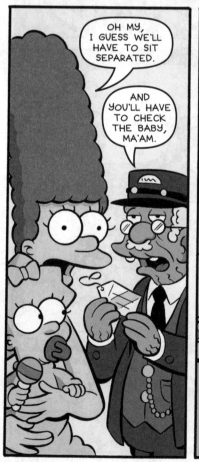

OH MY, I GUESS WE'LL HAVE TO SIT SEPARATED.

AND YOU'LL HAVE TO CHECK THE BABY, MA'AM.

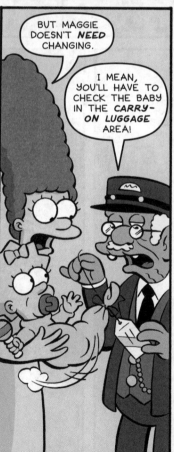

BUT MAGGIE DOESN'T *NEED* CHANGING.

I MEAN, YOU'LL HAVE TO CHECK THE BABY IN THE *CARRY-ON LUGGAGE* AREA!

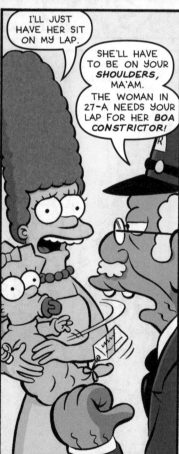

I'LL JUST HAVE HER SIT ON MY LAP.

SHE'LL HAVE TO BE ON YOUR *SHOULDERS*, MA'AM. THE WOMAN IN 27-A NEEDS YOUR LAP FOR HER *BOA CONSTRICTOR!*

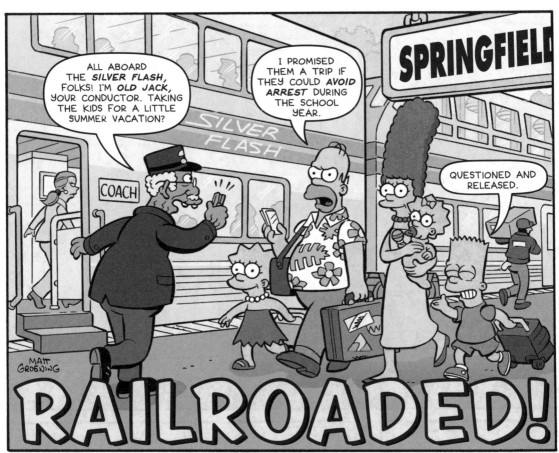

ALL ABOARD THE *SILVER FLASH*, FOLKS! I'M *OLD JACK*, YOUR CONDUCTOR. TAKING THE KIDS FOR A LITTLE SUMMER VACATION?

I PROMISED THEM A TRIP IF THEY COULD *AVOID ARREST* DURING THE SCHOOL YEAR.

QUESTIONED AND RELEASED.

SPRINGFIELD

SILVER FLASH

COACH

MATT GROENING

RAILROADED!

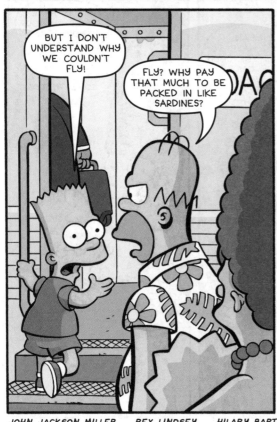

BUT I DON'T UNDERSTAND WHY WE COULDN'T FLY!

FLY? WHY PAY THAT MUCH TO BE PACKED IN LIKE SARDINES?

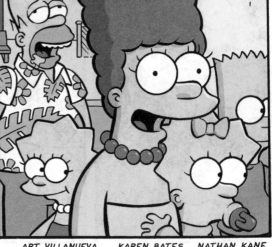

COME ON, KIDS. WE CAN PRETEND WE'RE IN THE OLD WEST...OR *MODERN EUROPE!*

BESIDES, ON THE TRAIN WE'LL BE ABLE TO...

MMM... SARDINES.

RIDE THE RAILS

WHAT'S YOUR HURRY, SONNY?

JOHN JACKSON MILLER
SCRIPT

REX LINDSEY
PENCILS

HILARY BARTA
INKS

ART VILLANUEVA
COLORS

KAREN BATES
LETTERS

NATHAN KANE
EDITOR
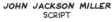

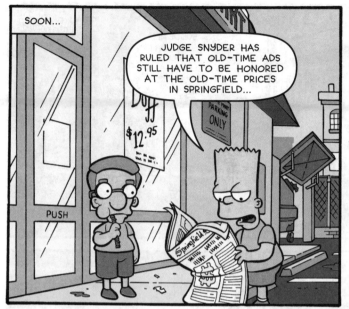

SOON...

JUDGE SNYDER HAS RULED THAT OLD-TIME ADS STILL HAVE TO BE HONORED AT THE OLD-TIME PRICES IN SPRINGFIELD...

PUSH

$12.95

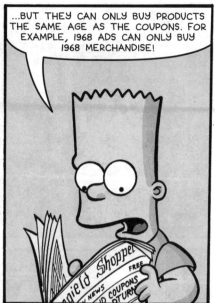

...BUT THEY CAN ONLY BUY PRODUCTS THE SAME AGE AS THE COUPONS. FOR EXAMPLE, 1968 ADS CAN ONLY BUY 1968 MERCHANDISE!

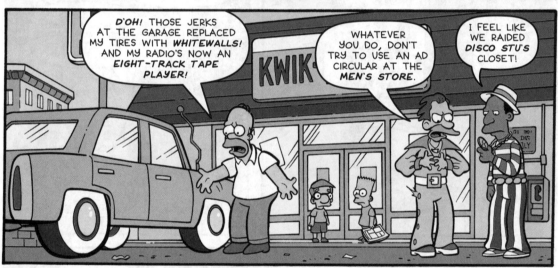

D'OH! THOSE JERKS AT THE GARAGE REPLACED MY TIRES WITH *WHITEWALLS!* AND MY RADIO'S NOW AN *EIGHT-TRACK TAPE PLAYER!*

WHATEVER YOU DO, DON'T TRY TO USE AN AD CIRCULAR AT THE *MEN'S STORE.*

I FEEL LIKE WE RAIDED *DISCO STU'S* CLOSET!

KWIK

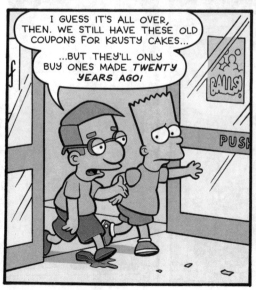

I GUESS IT'S ALL OVER, THEN. WE STILL HAVE THESE OLD COUPONS FOR KRUSTY CAKES...

...BUT THEY'LL ONLY BUY ONES MADE *TWENTY YEARS AGO!*

PUSH

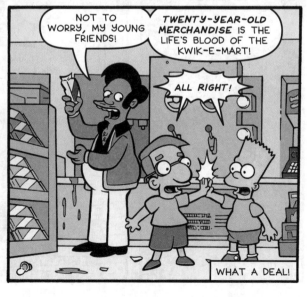

NOT TO WORRY, MY YOUNG FRIENDS!

TWENTY-YEAR-OLD MERCHANDISE IS THE LIFE'S BLOOD OF THE KWIK-E-MART!

ALL RIGHT!

WHAT A DEAL!

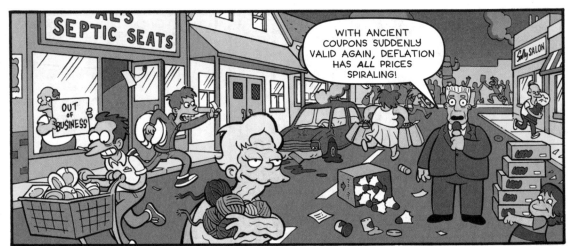

WITH ANCIENT COUPONS SUDDENLY VALID AGAIN, DEFLATION HAS *ALL* PRICES SPIRALING!

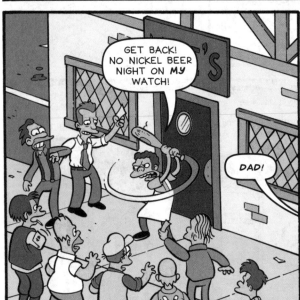

GET BACK! NO NICKEL BEER NIGHT ON *MY* WATCH!

DAD!

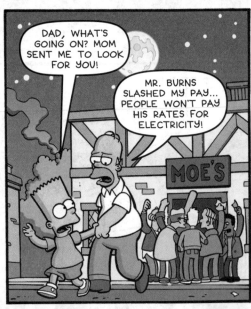

DAD, WHAT'S GOING ON? MOM SENT ME TO LOOK FOR YOU!

MR. BURNS SLASHED MY PAY... PEOPLE WON'T PAY HIS RATES FOR ELECTRICITY!

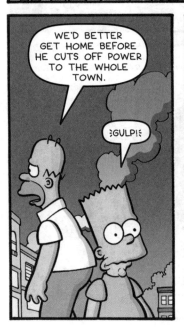

WE'D BETTER GET HOME BEFORE HE CUTS OFF POWER TO THE WHOLE TOWN.

¡GULP!¿

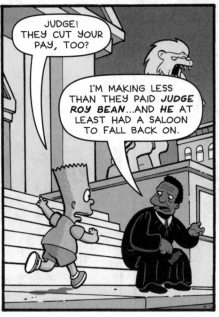

JUDGE! THEY CUT YOUR PAY, TOO?

I'M MAKING LESS THAN THEY PAID *JUDGE ROY BEAN*...AND *HE* AT LEAST HAD A SALOON TO FALL BACK ON.

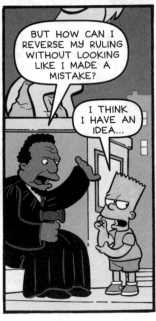

BUT HOW CAN I REVERSE MY RULING WITHOUT LOOKING LIKE I MADE A MISTAKE?

I THINK I HAVE AN IDEA...

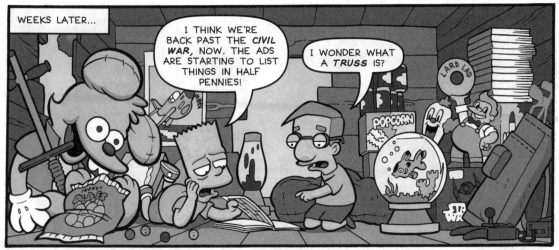

WEEKS LATER...

I THINK WE'RE BACK PAST THE *CIVIL WAR*, NOW. THE ADS ARE STARTING TO LIST THINGS IN HALF PENNIES!

I WONDER WHAT A *TRUSS* IS?

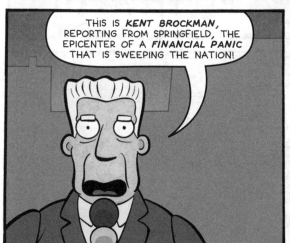

THIS IS *KENT BROCKMAN*, REPORTING FROM SPRINGFIELD, THE EPICENTER OF A *FINANCIAL PANIC* THAT IS SWEEPING THE NATION!

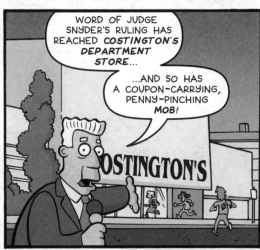

WORD OF JUDGE SNYDER'S RULING HAS REACHED *COSTINGTON'S DEPARTMENT STORE*...

...AND SO HAS A COUPON-CARRYING, PENNY-PINCHING *MOB*!

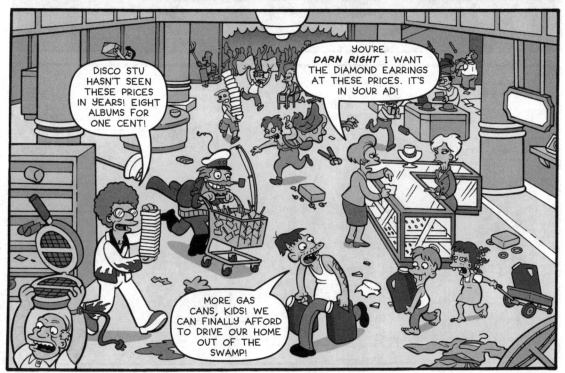

DISCO STU HASN'T SEEN THESE PRICES IN YEARS! EIGHT ALBUMS FOR ONE CENT!

YOU'RE *DARN RIGHT* I WANT THE DIAMOND EARRINGS AT THESE PRICES. IT'S IN YOUR AD!

MORE GAS CANS, KIDS! WE CAN FINALLY AFFORD TO DRIVE OUR HOME OUT OF THE SWAMP!

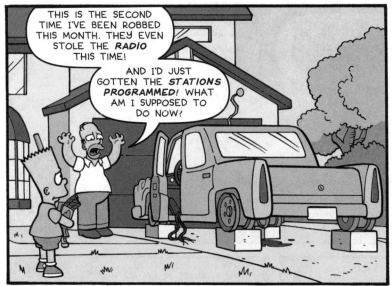

THIS IS THE SECOND TIME I'VE BEEN ROBBED THIS MONTH. THEY EVEN STOLE THE *RADIO* THIS TIME!

AND I'D JUST GOTTEN THE *STATIONS PROGRAMMED!* WHAT AM I SUPPOSED TO DO NOW?

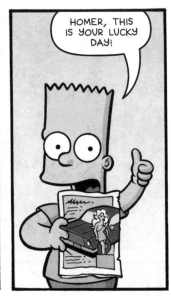

HOMER, THIS IS YOUR LUCKY DAY!

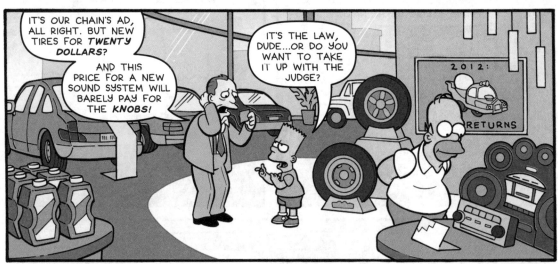

IT'S OUR CHAIN'S AD, ALL RIGHT. BUT NEW TIRES FOR *TWENTY DOLLARS*?

AND THIS PRICE FOR A NEW SOUND SYSTEM WILL BARELY PAY FOR THE *KNOBS!*

IT'S THE LAW, DUDE...OR DO YOU WANT TO TAKE IT UP WITH THE JUDGE?

2012: M RETURNS

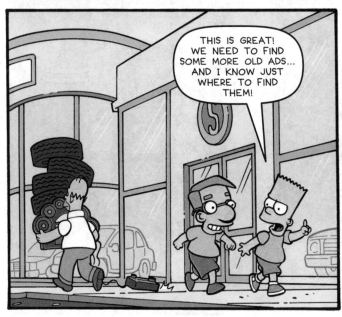

THIS IS GREAT! WE NEED TO FIND SOME MORE OLD ADS... AND I KNOW JUST WHERE TO FIND THEM!

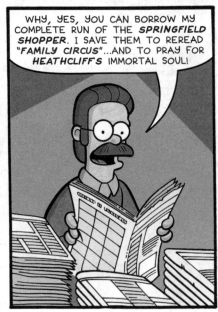

WHY, YES, YOU CAN BORROW MY COMPLETE RUN OF THE *SPRINGFIELD SHOPPER*. I SAVE THEM TO REREAD *"FAMILY CIRCUS"*...AND TO PRAY FOR *HEATHCLIFF'S* IMMORTAL SOUL!

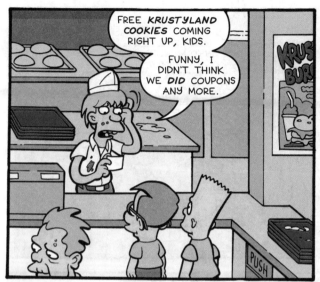

FREE *KRUSTYLAND COOKIES* COMING RIGHT UP, KIDS.

FUNNY, I DIDN'T THINK WE *DID* COUPONS ANY MORE.

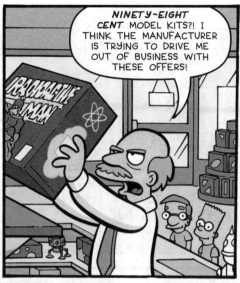

NINETY-EIGHT CENT MODEL KITS?! I THINK THE MANUFACTURER IS TRYING TO DRIVE ME OUT OF BUSINESS WITH THESE OFFERS!

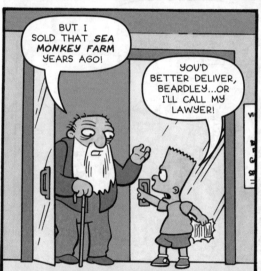

BUT I SOLD THAT *SEA MONKEY FARM* YEARS AGO!

YOU'D BETTER DELIVER, BEARDLEY...OR I'LL CALL MY LAWYER!

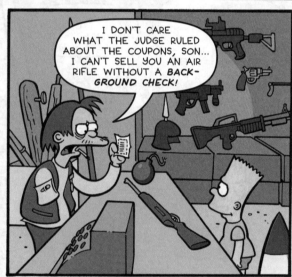

I DON'T CARE WHAT THE JUDGE RULED ABOUT THE COUPONS, SON... I CAN'T SELL YOU AN AIR RIFLE WITHOUT A *BACK-GROUND CHECK!*

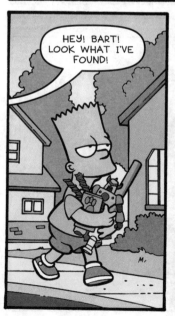

HEY! BART! LOOK WHAT I'VE FOUND!

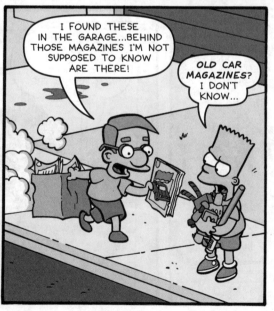

I FOUND THESE IN THE GARAGE...BEHIND THOSE MAGAZINES I'M NOT SUPPOSED TO KNOW ARE THERE!

OLD CAR MAGAZINES? I DON'T KNOW...

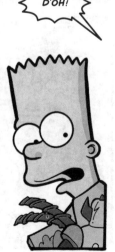

D'OH!

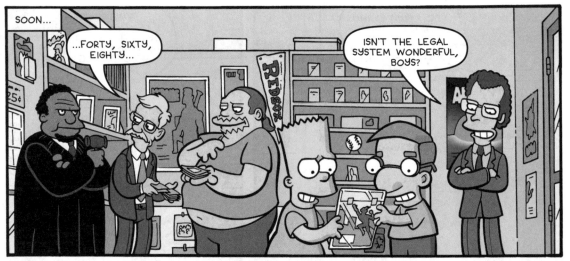

SOON...

...FORTY, SIXTY, EIGHTY...

ISN'T THE LEGAL SYSTEM WONDERFUL, BOYS?

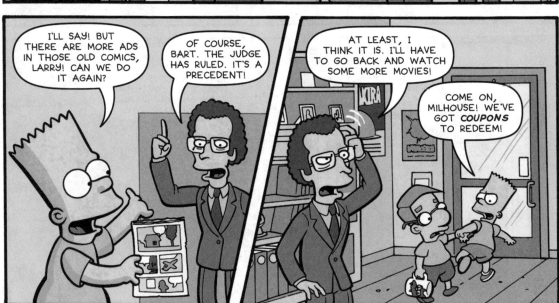

I'LL SAY! BUT THERE ARE MORE ADS IN THOSE OLD COMICS, LARRY! CAN WE DO IT AGAIN?

OF COURSE, BART. THE JUDGE HAS RULED. IT'S A PRECEDENT!

AT LEAST, I THINK IT IS. I'LL HAVE TO GO BACK AND WATCH SOME MORE MOVIES!

COME ON, MILHOUSE! WE'VE GOT *COUPONS* TO REDEEM!

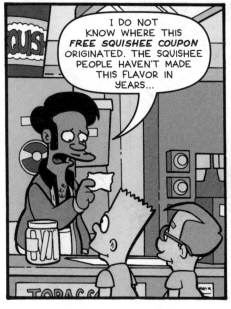

I DO NOT KNOW WHERE THIS *FREE SQUISHEE COUPON* ORIGINATED. THE SQUISHEE PEOPLE HAVEN'T MADE THIS FLAVOR IN YEARS...

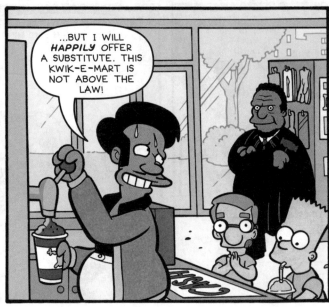

...BUT I WILL *HAPPILY* OFFER A SUBSTITUTE. THIS KWIK-E-MART IS NOT ABOVE THE LAW!

WEEKS LATER...
"DEAR KID. ARE YOU KIDDING? WE DON'T EVEN HAVE THIS COMIC BOOK ANYMORE!
P.S. YOU MUST BE STUPID, STUPID, STUPID!"
I CAN'T BELIEVE THEY'D TALK TO A CUSTOMER THAT WAY!
BELIEVE IT, MILHOUSE! I'M SO MAD I COULD SUE!
SUE, YOU SAY? LARRY H. LAWYER HERE. NORMALLY YOU HAVE TO SAY MY NAME THREE TIMES FOR ME TO APPEAR, BUT I LOST TRACK OF THE AMBULANCE I WAS CHASING.
HERE'S MY CARD, YOUNG MAN!
LV-426
YOU CAN SUE OVER AN INSULTING LETTER?
I DON'T KNOW... BUT I SAW IT DONE IN A JOHN GRISHAM FILM ONCE.
IF IT WORKED FOR MATT DAMON, IT CAN WORK FOR US!
AT TRIAL...
NO EXPIRATION DATE! NO "WHILE SUPPLIES LAST!"
IT LOOKS CLEAR-CUT TO ME! THIS COURT RULES THAT THE PUBLISHER MUST MAKE GOOD ON THE OFFER!
BUT, YOUR HONOR! WE DIDN'T KEEP ANY COPIES OF THAT BOOK!
YOUR COMPANY SHOULD HAVE THOUGHT OF THAT BEFORE YOU LOST MY COPY IN THE MAIL YEARS AGO. FIND THEM A COPY!
REVENGE IS ADJOURNED!
WHACK!

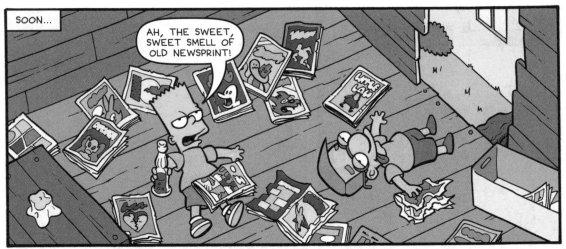

SOON...

AH, THE SWEET, SWEET SMELL OF OLD NEWSPRINT!

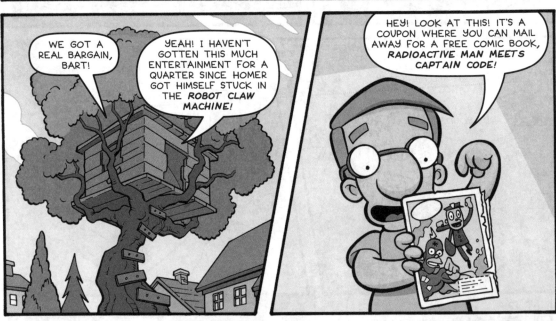

WE GOT A REAL BARGAIN, BART!

YEAH! I HAVEN'T GOTTEN THIS MUCH ENTERTAINMENT FOR A QUARTER SINCE HOMER GOT HIMSELF STUCK IN THE *ROBOT CLAW MACHINE!*

HEY! LOOK AT THIS! IT'S A COUPON WHERE YOU CAN MAIL AWAY FOR A FREE COMIC BOOK, *RADIOACTIVE MAN MEETS CAPTAIN CODE!*

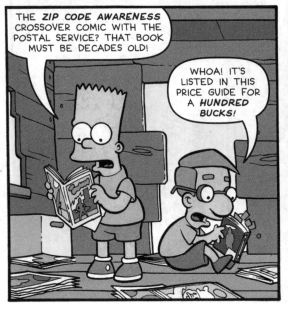

THE *ZIP CODE AWARENESS* CROSSOVER COMIC WITH THE POSTAL SERVICE? THAT BOOK MUST BE DECADES OLD!

WHOA! IT'S LISTED IN THIS PRICE GUIDE FOR A *HUNDRED BUCKS!*

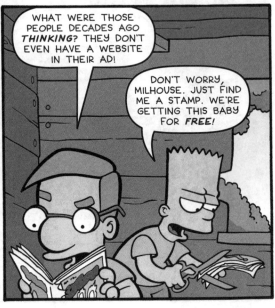

WHAT WERE THOSE PEOPLE DECADES AGO *THINKING*? THEY DON'T EVEN HAVE A WEBSITE IN THEIR AD!

DON'T WORRY, MILHOUSE. JUST FIND ME A STAMP. WE'RE GETTING THIS BABY FOR *FREE!*

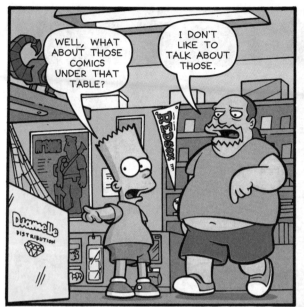

WELL, WHAT ABOUT THOSE COMICS UNDER THAT TABLE?

I DON'T LIKE TO TALK ABOUT THOSE.

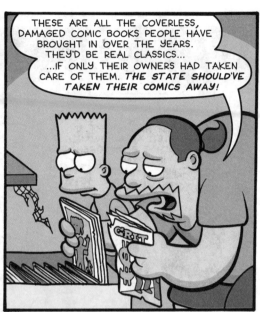

THESE ARE ALL THE COVERLESS, DAMAGED COMIC BOOKS PEOPLE HAVE BROUGHT IN OVER THE YEARS. THEY'D BE REAL CLASSICS...

...IF ONLY THEIR OWNERS HAD TAKEN CARE OF THEM. *THE STATE SHOULD'VE TAKEN THEIR COMICS AWAY!*

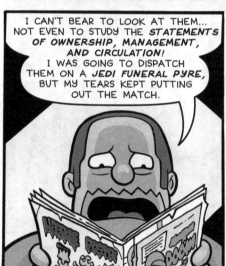

I CAN'T BEAR TO LOOK AT THEM... NOT EVEN TO STUDY THE *STATEMENTS OF OWNERSHIP, MANAGEMENT, AND CIRCULATION!* I WAS GOING TO DISPATCH THEM ON A *JEDI FUNERAL PYRE,* BUT MY TEARS KEPT PUTTING OUT THE MATCH.

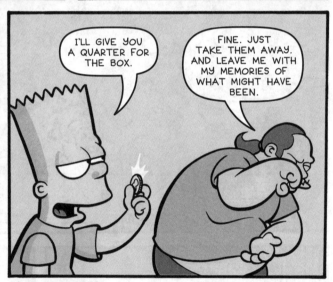

I'LL GIVE YOU A QUARTER FOR THE BOX.

FINE. JUST TAKE THEM AWAY. AND LEAVE ME WITH MY MEMORIES OF WHAT MIGHT HAVE BEEN.

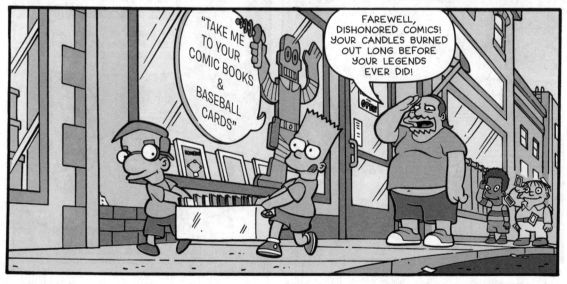

"TAKE ME TO YOUR COMIC BOOKS & BASEBALL CARDS"

FAREWELL, DISHONORED COMICS! YOUR CANDLES BURNED OUT LONG BEFORE YOUR LEGENDS EVER DID!

FOR A LIMITED TIME ONLY

I DON'T KNOW WHAT YOU EXPECT TO BUY HERE, BART. NEITHER ONE OF US HAS GOTTEN AN ALLOWANCE SINCE THAT *BLOWTORCH INCIDENT!*

DON'T WORRY, MILHOUSE. IT'S A COMICS SHOP. THERE'S ALWAYS THE *QUARTER BOXES!*

MATT GROENING

A DOLLAR EACH?! *AYE, CARUMBA!* WHAT HAPPENED?

NEW LOW PRICE!

1$ ea.!

THOSE ARE THE COMICS NO ONE WANTS. YOU HAD THEM PRICED AT A *QUARTER* EACH!

THEY ARE NOW *DOLLAR* BOXES, AS YOU CAN PLAINLY SEE. WELCOME TO THE "NEW NORMAL."

JOHN JACKSON MILLER
SCRIPT

JAMES LLOYD
PENCILS

ANDREW PEPOY
INKS

NATHAN HAMILL
COLORS

KAREN BATES
LETTERS

NATHAN KANE
EDITOR

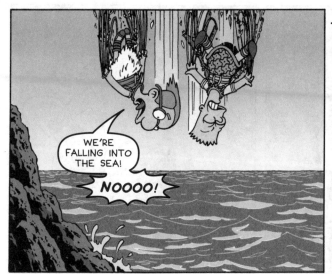

WE'RE FALLING INTO THE SEA!

NOOOO!

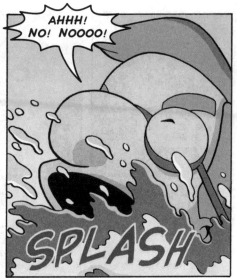

AHHH! NO! NOOOO!

SPLASH

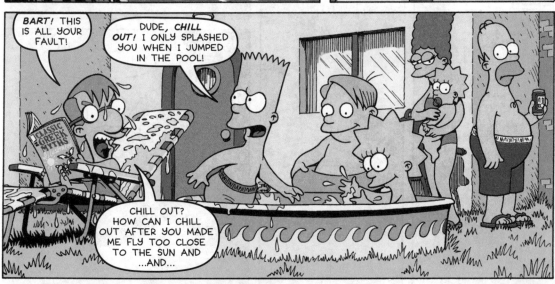

BART! THIS IS ALL YOUR FAULT!

DUDE, CHILL OUT! I ONLY SPLASHED YOU WHEN I JUMPED IN THE POOL!

CHILL OUT? HOW CAN I CHILL OUT AFTER YOU MADE ME FLY TOO CLOSE TO THE SUN AND ...AND...

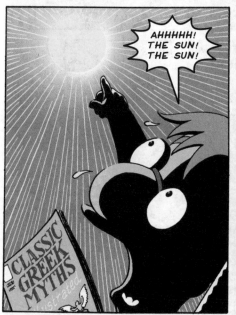

AHHHHH! THE SUN! THE SUN!

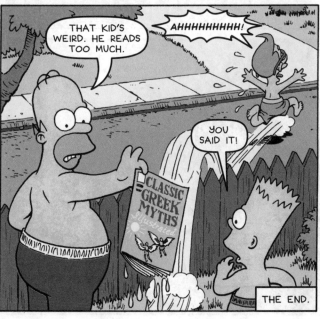

THAT KID'S WEIRD. HE READS TOO MUCH.

AHHHHHHHHH!

YOU SAID IT!

THE END.

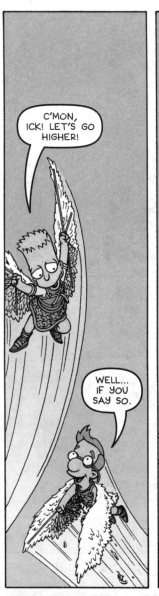

C'MON, ICK! LET'S GO HIGHER!

WELL... IF YOU SAY SO.

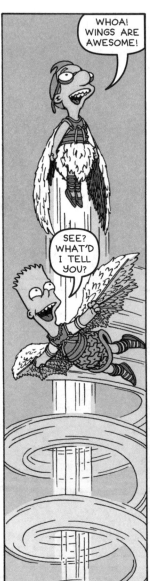

WHOA! WINGS ARE AWESOME!

SEE? WHAT'D I TELL YOU?

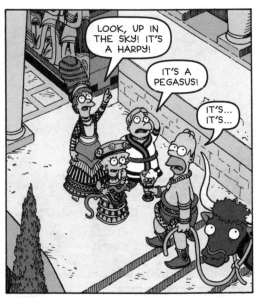

LOOK, UP IN THE SKY! IT'S A HARPY!

IT'S A PEGASUS!

IT'S... IT'S...

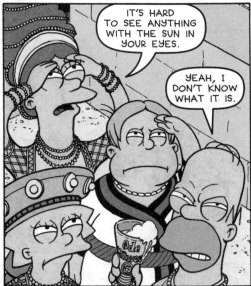

IT'S HARD TO SEE ANYTHING WITH THE SUN IN YOUR EYES.

YEAH, I DON'T KNOW WHAT IT IS.

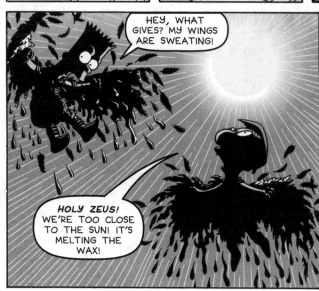

HEY, WHAT GIVES? MY WINGS ARE SWEATING!

HOLY ZEUS! WE'RE TOO CLOSE TO THE SUN! IT'S MELTING THE WAX!

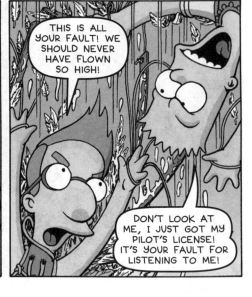

THIS IS ALL YOUR FAULT! WE SHOULD NEVER HAVE FLOWN SO HIGH!

DON'T LOOK AT ME, I JUST GOT MY PILOT'S LICENSE! IT'S YOUR FAULT FOR LISTENING TO ME!

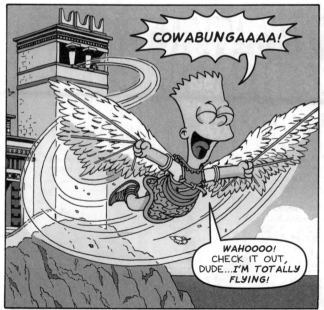

COWABUNGAAAA!

WAHOOOO! CHECK IT OUT, DUDE...*I'M TOTALLY FLYING!*

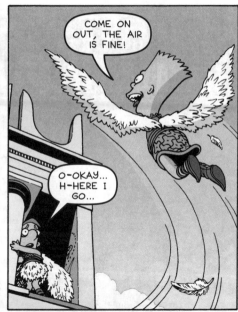

COME ON OUT, THE AIR IS FINE!

O-OKAY... H-HERE I GO...

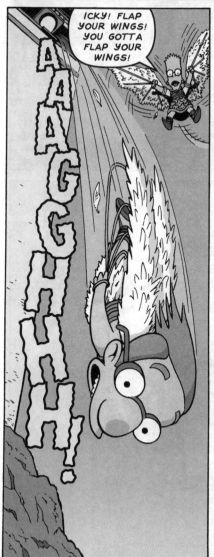

ICKY! FLAP YOUR WINGS! YOU GOTTA FLAP YOUR WINGS!

AAAGGGHHH!

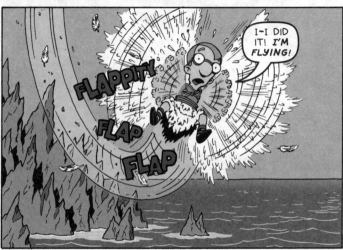

FLAPPITY FLAP N FLAP

I-I DID IT! *I'M FLYING!*

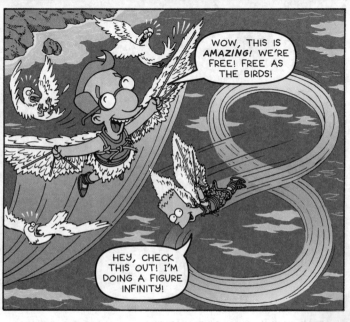

WOW, THIS IS *AMAZING!* WE'RE FREE! FREE AS THE BIRDS!

HEY, CHECK THIS OUT! I'M DOING A FIGURE INFINITY!

FLIGHT OF FANTASY

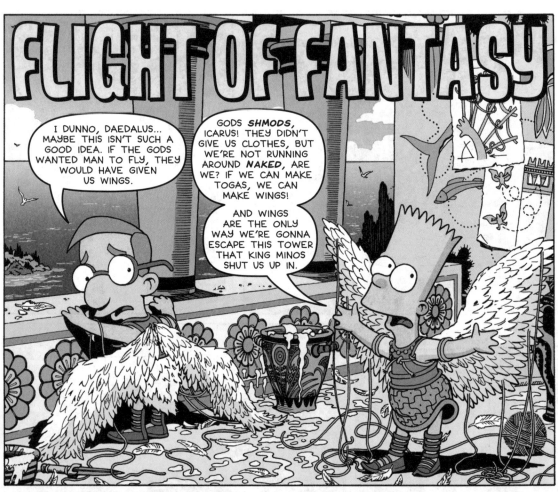

I DUNNO, DAEDALUS... MAYBE THIS ISN'T SUCH A GOOD IDEA. IF THE GODS WANTED MAN TO FLY, THEY WOULD HAVE GIVEN US WINGS.

GODS *SHMODS*, ICARUS! THEY DIDN'T GIVE US CLOTHES, BUT WE'RE NOT RUNNING AROUND *NAKED*, ARE WE? IF WE CAN MAKE TOGAS, WE CAN MAKE WINGS!

AND WINGS ARE THE ONLY WAY WE'RE GONNA ESCAPE THIS TOWER THAT KING MINOS SHUT US UP IN.

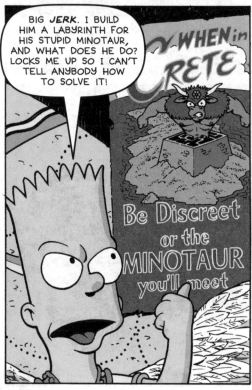

BIG *JERK*. I BUILD HIM A LABYRINTH FOR HIS STUPID MINOTAUR, AND WHAT DOES HE DO? LOCKS ME UP SO I CAN'T TELL ANYBODY HOW TO SOLVE IT!

WHEN in CRETE

Be Discreet or the MINOTAUR you'll meet

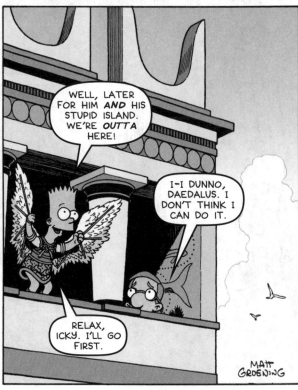

WELL, LATER FOR HIM *AND* HIS STUPID ISLAND. WE'RE *OUTTA* HERE!

I-I DUNNO, DAEDALUS. I DON'T THINK I CAN DO IT.

RELAX, ICKY. I'LL GO FIRST.

MATT GROENING

EVAN DORKIN
STORY

ERIC SHANOWER
ART

ART VILLANUEVA
COLORS

KAREN BATES
LETTERS

NATHAN KANE
EDITOR

THAT NIGHT...
WHY AREN'T YOU EATING, HONEY?
NOW, MARGE, IF THE BOY DOESN'T WANT TO EAT, YOU CAN'T FORCE HIM!
I CAN'T EAT. I CAN'T SLEEP.
I NEED TO WIN HER OVER, BUT HOW?
YOINK!
DO YOU REALLY CARE ABOUT THIS GIRL, BART?
NO! I NEED TO BEAT NELSON!
BART, I WOULDN'T DO THIS. SOMETIMES WHEN TWO ALPHA MALES COMPETE, THEY BOTH LOSE THEIR DOMAIN.
ALSO, DESPITE HIS ROUGH EXTERIOR, NELSON HAS SOME HIDDEN SOFTNESS THAT SOME GIRLS FIND VERY ATTRACTIVE.
IN FACT, HE ONCE TOLD ME SOMETHING THAT NO ONE ELSE KNOWS ABOUT HIM!
OH REALLY?

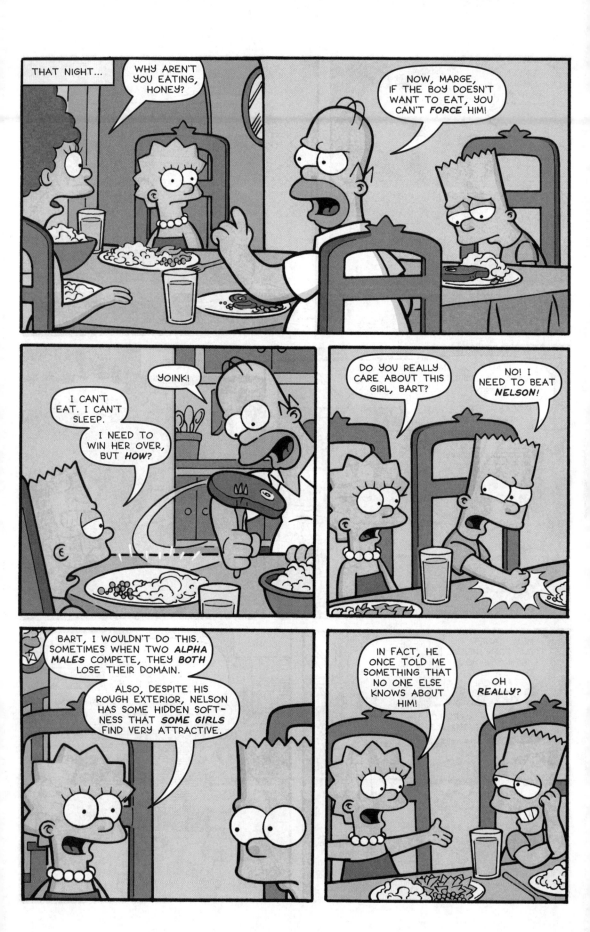

EAT MY SHORTS, GRAVITY!
OOOH! HE MIGHT GET INTO ORBIT!
NAILED IT! LET'S SEE ANYONE *ELSE* TRY THAT!
READY FOR AN AWESOME DISPLAY OF BRUTE STRENGTH, JANET? HOPE YOUR SEAT IS COMFY. BECAUSE THIS COULD TAKE A WHILE.
MILK
2.7 SECONDS LATER...
NEXT!
OWW! *MY ULNA!*
HEY, JANET. I STOLE SOME NERD'S LUNCH FOR YOU. THERE'S EXTRA TAPIOCA!
HMMM...
I'M ALLERGIC, BUT THANKS!
SOON...
HEY, JANET. I STOLE SOME NERD'S HOMEWORK FOR YOU. YOU'LL NEVER HAVE TO DO FRACTIONS AGAIN!
D'OH!

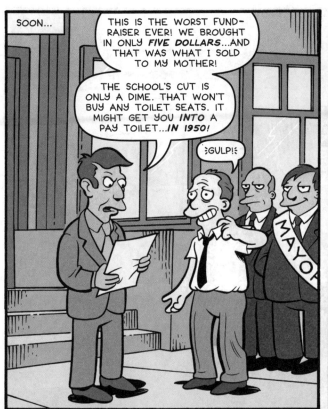

SOON...

THIS IS THE WORST FUND-RAISER EVER! WE BROUGHT IN ONLY *FIVE DOLLARS*...AND THAT WAS WHAT I SOLD TO MY MOTHER!

THE SCHOOL'S CUT IS ONLY A DIME. THAT WON'T BUY ANY TOILET SEATS. IT MIGHT GET YOU *INTO* A PAY TOILET...*IN 1950!*

¿GULP!¿

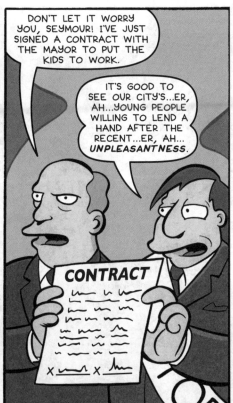

DON'T LET IT WORRY YOU, SEYMOUR! I'VE JUST SIGNED A CONTRACT WITH THE MAYOR TO PUT THE KIDS TO WORK.

IT'S GOOD TO SEE OUR CITY'S...ER, AH...YOUNG PEOPLE WILLING TO LEND A HAND AFTER THE RECENT...ER, AH... *UNPLEASANTNESS.*

CONTRACT

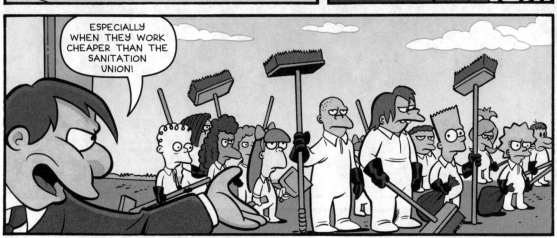

ESPECIALLY WHEN THEY WORK CHEAPER THAN THE SANITATION UNION!

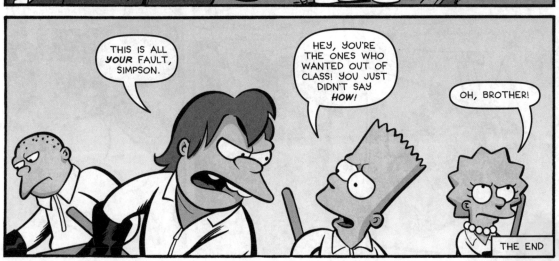

THIS IS ALL *YOUR* FAULT, SIMPSON.

HEY, YOU'RE THE ONES WHO WANTED OUT OF CLASS! YOU JUST DIDN'T SAY *HOW!*

OH, BROTHER!

THE END

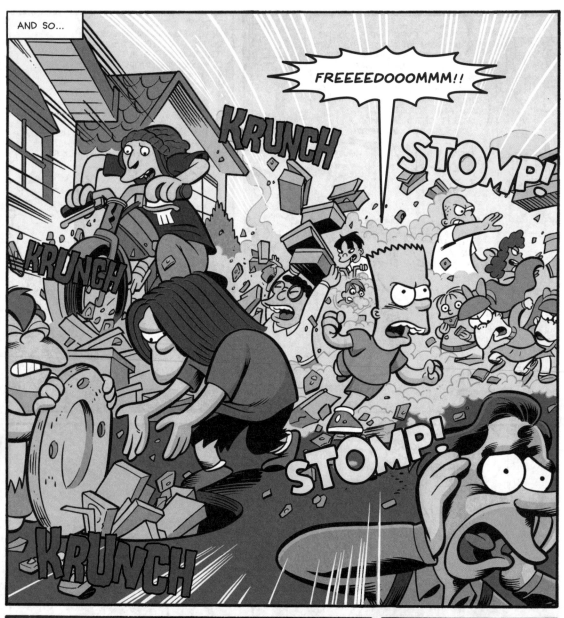

AND SO...

FREEEEDOOOMMM!!

KRUNCH

STOMP!

KRUNCH

STOMP!

KRUNCH

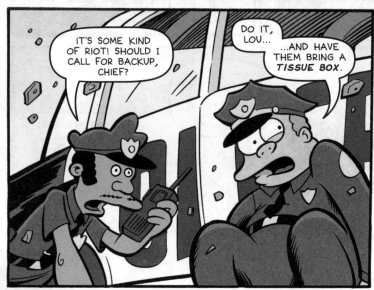

IT'S SOME KIND OF RIOT! SHOULD I CALL FOR BACKUP, CHIEF?

DO IT, LOU...

...AND HAVE THEM BRING A *TISSUE BOX*.

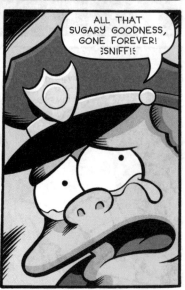

ALL THAT SUGARY GOODNESS, GONE FOREVER! ⸝SNIFF!⸜

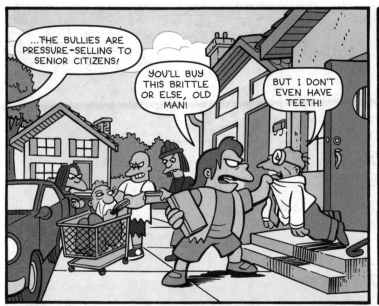

...THE BULLIES ARE PRESSURE-SELLING TO SENIOR CITIZENS!

YOU'LL BUY THIS BRITTLE OR ELSE, OLD MAN!

BUT I DON'T EVEN HAVE TEETH!

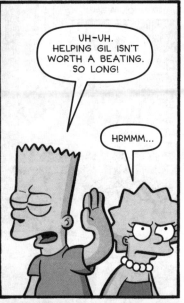

UH-UH. HELPING GIL ISN'T WORTH A BEATING. SO LONG!

HRMMM...

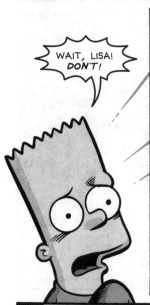

WAIT, LISA! DON'T!

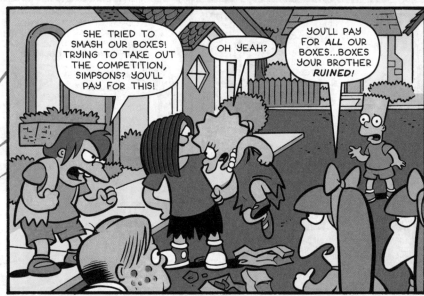

SHE TRIED TO SMASH OUR BOXES! TRYING TO TAKE OUT THE COMPETITION, SIMPSONS? YOU'LL PAY FOR THIS!

OH YEAH?

YOU'LL PAY FOR ALL OUR BOXES...BOXES YOUR BROTHER RUINED!

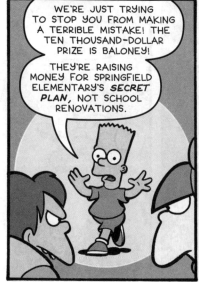

WE'RE JUST TRYING TO STOP YOU FROM MAKING A TERRIBLE MISTAKE! THE TEN THOUSAND-DOLLAR PRIZE IS BALONEY!

THEY'RE RAISING MONEY FOR SPRINGFIELD ELEMENTARY'S SECRET PLAN, NOT SCHOOL RENOVATIONS.

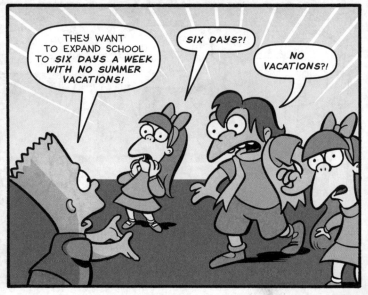

THEY WANT TO EXPAND SCHOOL TO SIX DAYS A WEEK WITH NO SUMMER VACATIONS!

SIX DAYS?!

NO VACATIONS?!

AND SOON AGAIN...
DADDY!
SURE, KID. THESE GUYS WILL BUY EVERYTHING YOU'VE GOT. I FORGOT TO PICK UP MY **GOVERNMENT CHEESE DOODLES** THIS MONTH!
OH, HI, MILHOUSE! I'M GLAD TO SEE YOU'RE SELLING TO THESE NICE MEN.
WHAT'S UP, LISA?
I COMMEND YOU ON THE CHOICE YOU'RE MAKING, MOE. THIS IS A SUPER-HEALTHY, ZERO-CAL MIX OF **ORGANIC LEGUMES!**
LEGUMES? I THOUGHT THIS WAS GOOD OLD AMERICAN **JUNK FOOD!** YOU CAN KEEP 'EM!
C'MON, GUYS... THERE'S STILL SOME **CHIP GUT** AT THE BOTTOM OF THE SNACK MACHINE!
YOU RUINED MY SALE, LISA! HOW COULD YOU?
YOU DON'T HAVE TO DO THAT, BART! I ALREADY STOPPED THE SALE!
WHO CARES? I LIKE THE SOUND THEY MAKE!
KRUNNCHH
KRUNNCHH
OH, NO! BART! LOOK OVER THERE...

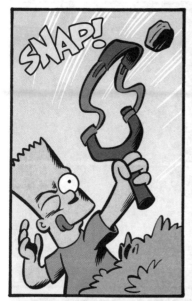

SNAP!

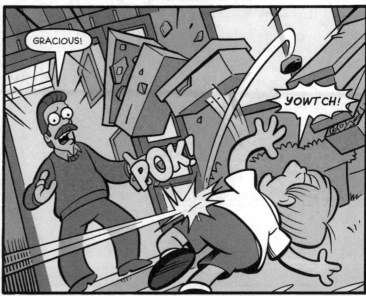

GRACIOUS!

YOWTCH!

POK!

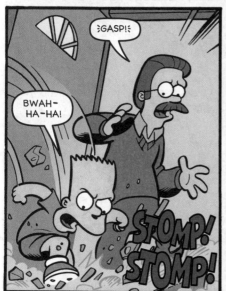

:GASP!:

BWAH-HA-HA!

STOMP! STOMP!

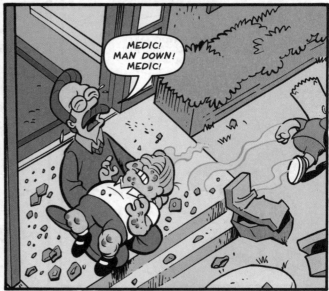

MEDIC! MAN DOWN! MEDIC!

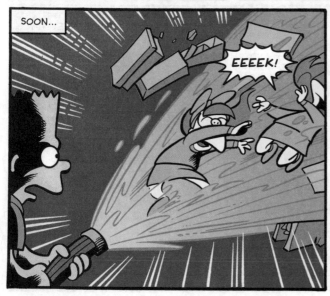

SOON...

EEEEK!

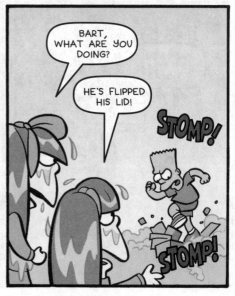

BART, WHAT ARE YOU DOING?

HE'S FLIPPED HIS LID!

STOMP!

STOMP!

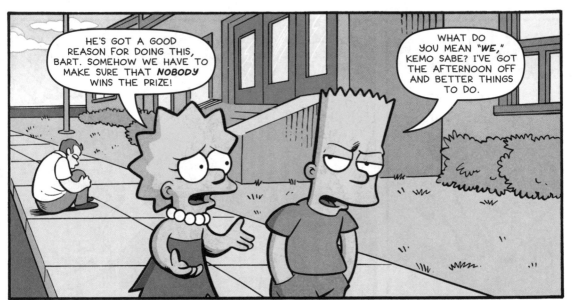

HE'S GOT A GOOD REASON FOR DOING THIS, BART. SOMEHOW WE HAVE TO MAKE SURE THAT *NOBODY* WINS THE PRIZE!

WHAT DO YOU MEAN *"WE,"* KEMO SABE? I'VE GOT THE AFTERNOON OFF AND BETTER THINGS TO DO.

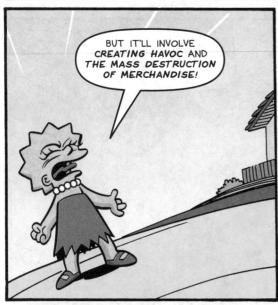

BUT IT'LL INVOLVE *CREATING HAVOC* AND *THE MASS DESTRUCTION OF MERCHANDISE!*

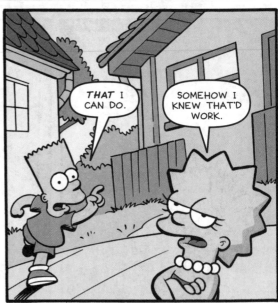

THAT I CAN DO.

SOMEHOW I KNEW THAT'D WORK.

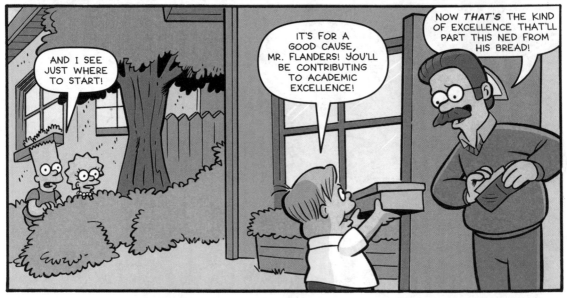

AND I SEE JUST WHERE TO START!

IT'S FOR A GOOD CAUSE, MR. FLANDERS! YOU'LL BE CONTRIBUTING TO ACADEMIC EXCELLENCE!

NOW *THAT'S* THE KIND OF EXCELLENCE THAT'LL PART THIS NED FROM HIS BREAD!

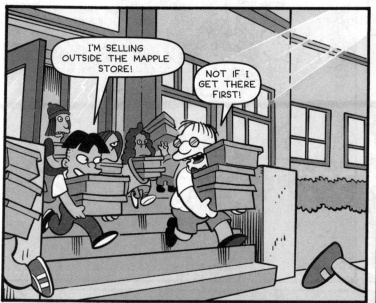

I'M SELLING OUTSIDE THE MAPPLE STORE!

NOT IF I GET THERE FIRST!

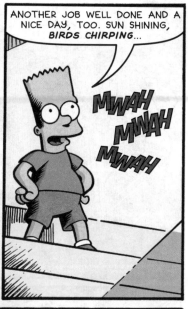

ANOTHER JOB WELL DONE AND A NICE DAY, TOO. SUN SHINING, *BIRDS CHIRPING*...

MWAH MWAH MWAH

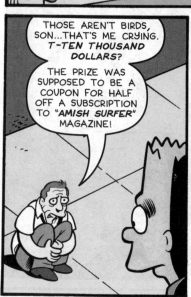

THOSE AREN'T BIRDS, SON...THAT'S ME CRYING. *T-TEN THOUSAND DOLLARS?*

THE PRIZE WAS SUPPOSED TO BE A COUPON FOR HALF OFF A SUBSCRIPTION TO "*AMISH SURFER*" MAGAZINE!

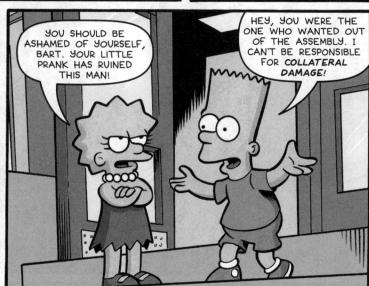

YOU SHOULD BE ASHAMED OF YOURSELF, BART. YOUR LITTLE PRANK HAS RUINED THIS MAN!

HEY, YOU WERE THE ONE WHO WANTED OUT OF THE ASSEMBLY. I CAN'T BE RESPONSIBLE FOR *COLLATERAL DAMAGE!*

AND YOU SHOULD BE ASHAMED, TOO. YOU GET KIDS TO *GUILT* PEOPLE INTO BUYING OVERPRICED, SECOND-RATE PRODUCTS...

...AND THE SCHOOL AND THE KIDS DON'T GET ANYTHING!

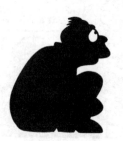

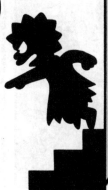

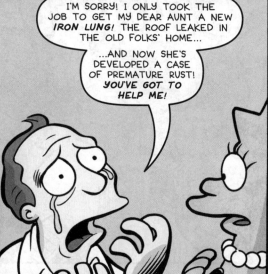

I'M SORRY! I ONLY TOOK THE JOB TO GET MY DEAR AUNT A NEW *IRON LUNG!* THE ROOF LEAKED IN THE OLD FOLKS' HOME...

...AND NOW SHE'S DEVELOPED A CASE OF PREMATURE RUST! *YOU'VE GOT TO HELP ME!*

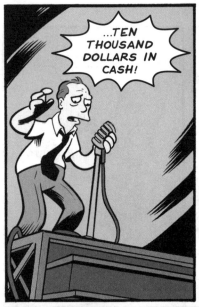

...TEN THOUSAND DOLLARS IN CASH!

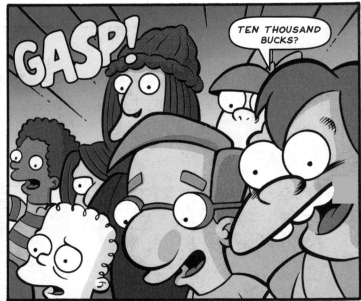

GASP!

TEN THOUSAND BUCKS?

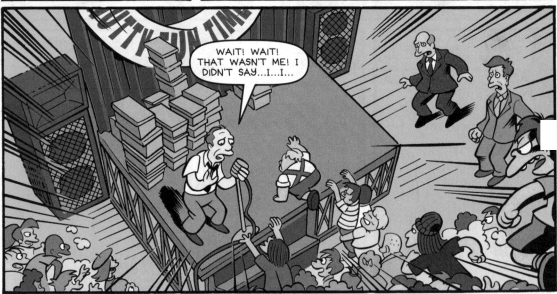

WAIT! WAIT! THAT WASN'T ME! I DIDN'T SAY...I...I...

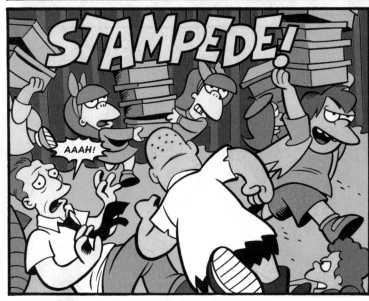

STAMPEDE!

AAAH!

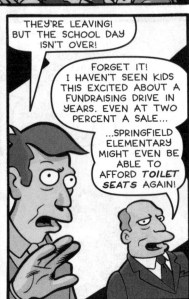

THEY'RE LEAVING! BUT THE SCHOOL DAY ISN'T OVER!

FORGET IT! I HAVEN'T SEEN KIDS THIS EXCITED ABOUT A FUNDRAISING DRIVE IN YEARS. EVEN AT TWO PERCENT A SALE...

...SPRINGFIELD ELEMENTARY MIGHT EVEN BE ABLE TO AFFORD TOILET SEATS AGAIN!

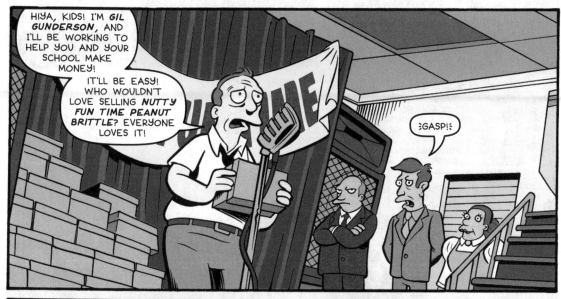

HIYA, KIDS! I'M *GIL GUNDERSON*, AND I'LL BE WORKING TO HELP YOU AND YOUR SCHOOL MAKE MONEY!

IT'LL BE EASY! WHO WOULDN'T LOVE SELLING *NUTTY FUN TIME PEANUT BRITTLE*? EVERYONE LOVES IT!

¡GASP!¡

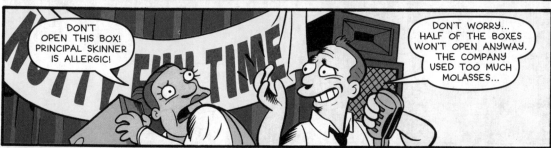

DON'T OPEN THIS BOX! PRINCIPAL SKINNER IS ALLERGIC!

DON'T WORRY... HALF OF THE BOXES WON'T OPEN ANYWAY. THE COMPANY USED TOO MUCH MOLASSES...

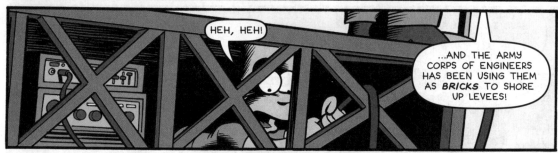

HEH, HEH!

...AND THE ARMY CORPS OF ENGINEERS HAS BEEN USING THEM AS *BRICKS* TO SHORE UP LEVEES!

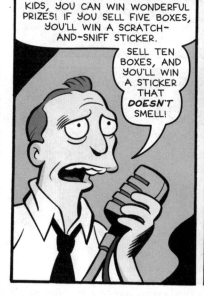

KIDS, YOU CAN WIN WONDERFUL PRIZES! IF YOU SELL FIVE BOXES, YOU'LL WIN A SCRATCH-AND-SNIFF STICKER.

SELL TEN BOXES, AND YOU'LL WIN A STICKER THAT *DOESN'T* SMELL!

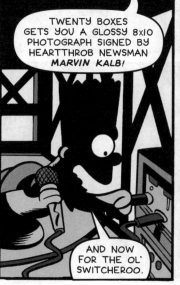

TWENTY BOXES GETS YOU A GLOSSY 8x10 PHOTOGRAPH SIGNED BY HEARTTHROB NEWSMAN *MARVIN KALB!*

AND NOW FOR THE OL' SWITCHEROO.

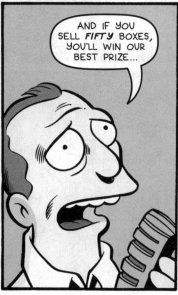

AND IF YOU SELL *FIFTY* BOXES, YOU'LL WIN OUR BEST PRIZE...

FUND-RAZING

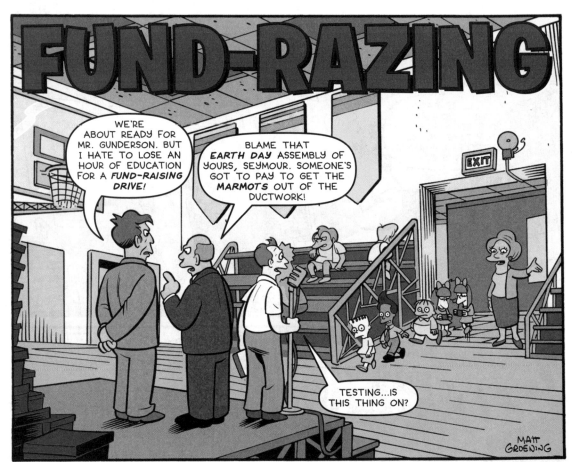

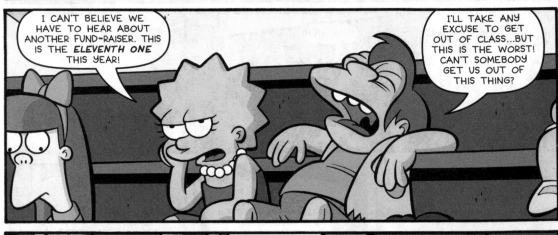

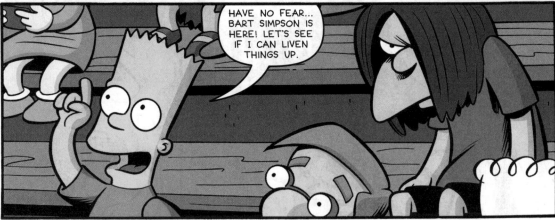

JOHN JACKSON MILLER SCRIPT   **JOHN DELANEY** PENCILS   **ANDREW PEPOY** INKS   **ART VILLANUEVA** COLORS   **KAREN BATES** LETTERS   **NATHAN KANE** EDITOR

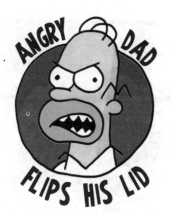

ANGRY DAD FLIPS HIS LID

by BART SIMPSON

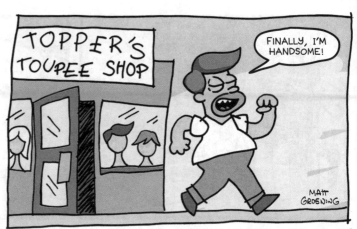

TOPPER'S TOUPEE SHOP

FINALLY, I'M HANDSOME!

MATT GROENING

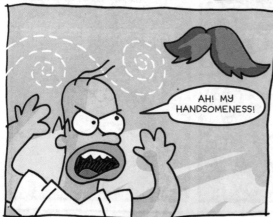

AH! MY HANDSOMENESS!

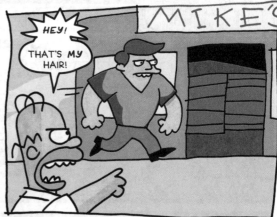

HEY! THAT'S MY HAIR!

MIKE'S

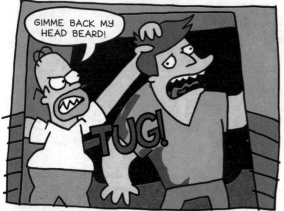

GIMME BACK MY HEAD BEARD!

TUG!

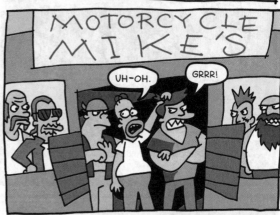

MOTORCYCLE MIKE'S

UH-OH.

GRRR!

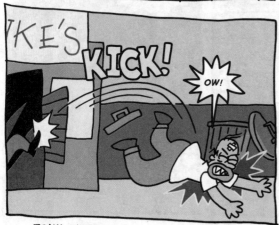

KE'S

KICK!

OW!

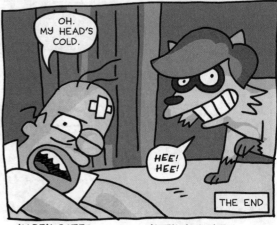

OH. MY HEAD'S COLD.

HEE! HEE!

THE END

TONY DIGEROLAMO SCRIPT

JASON HO ART

KAREN BATES LETTERS

NATHAN KANE EDITOR

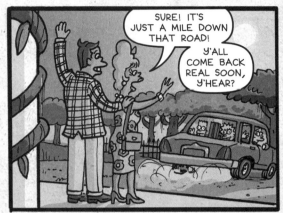

SURE! IT'S JUST A MILE DOWN THAT ROAD!

Y'ALL COME BACK REAL SOON, Y'HEAR?

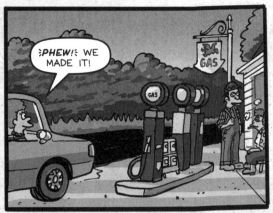

⦃PHEW!⦄ WE MADE IT!

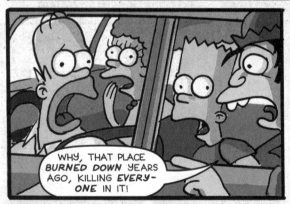

HOWDY, FOLKS! WHERE Y'ALL COMIN' FROM?

WE WERE JUST AT THE BIG HOUSE ON THE HILL.

IT WAS A CREEPFEST, MAN!

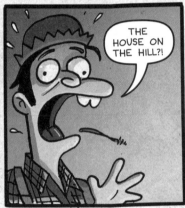

THE HOUSE ON THE HILL?!

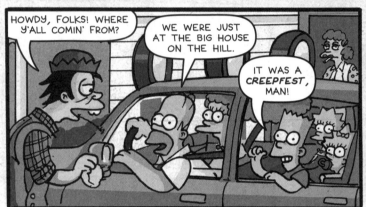

WHY, THAT PLACE BURNED DOWN YEARS AGO, KILLING EVERYONE IN IT!

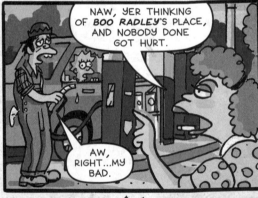

NAW, YER THINKING OF BOO RADLEY'S PLACE, AND NOBODY DONE GOT HURT.

AW, RIGHT...MY BAD.

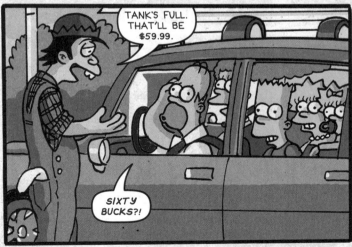

TANK'S FULL. THAT'LL BE $59.99.

SIXTY BUCKS?!

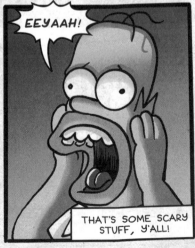

EEYAAH!

THAT'S SOME SCARY STUFF, Y'ALL!

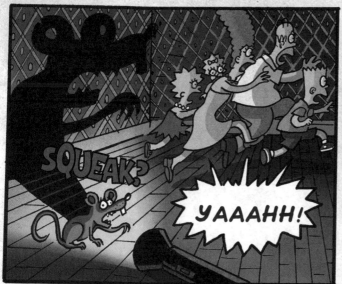

SQUEAK?

YAAAHH!

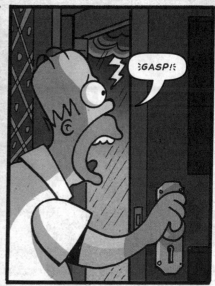

;GASP!;

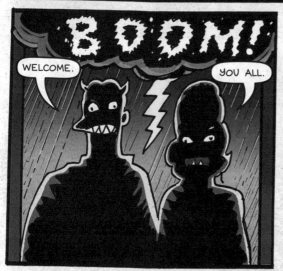

BOOM!

WELCOME.

YOU ALL.

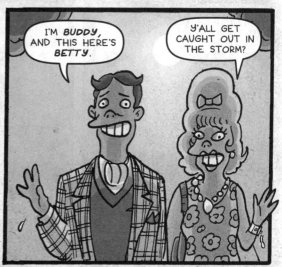

I'M BUDDY, AND THIS HERE'S BETTY.

Y'ALL GET CAUGHT OUT IN THE STORM?

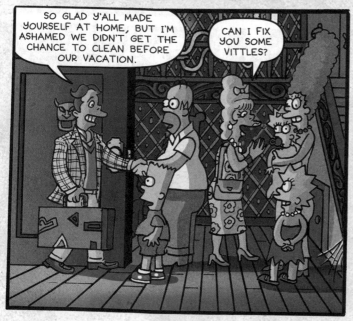

SO GLAD Y'ALL MADE YOURSELF AT HOME, BUT I'M ASHAMED WE DIDN'T GET THE CHANCE TO CLEAN BEFORE OUR VACATION.

CAN I FIX YOU SOME VITTLES?

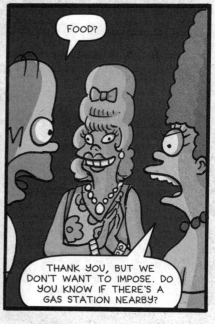

FOOD?

THANK YOU, BUT WE DON'T WANT TO IMPOSE. DO YOU KNOW IF THERE'S A GAS STATION NEARBY?

MOM!
MARGE!
H-HOMER? L-LISA?
OOF! WHAT ON EARTH?!
BUMP
I SAW A PAINTING WITH MOVING EYES!
THERE WASN'T ANY FOOD...
...AND I SAW A MONSTER!
LOOK! THERE IT IS!!
GASP!
I VONT TO SUCK YOUR BLOO--
WHY, YOU LITTLE...
ACK!
DAD... LOOK!
WHAT THE WHAT?!

M-MAYBE THERE ARE SOME BLANKETS IN HERE.
GASP!
BOY, THE ARTIST SURE CAPTURED THE EYES.
THEY'RE SO... REALISTIC!
EEK! THEY MOVED!
SQUEAK
SQUEAK
EEYAAH!

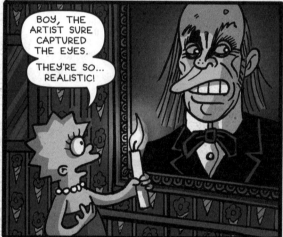

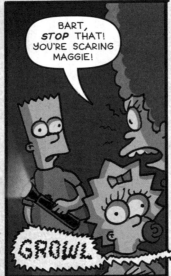

I VONT TO SUCK YOUR BLOOD!

BART, *STOP* THAT! YOU'RE SCARING MAGGIE!

GROWL

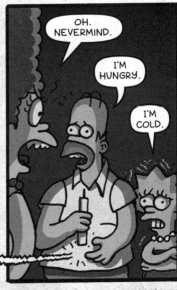

OH. NEVERMIND.

I'M HUNGRY.

I'M COLD.

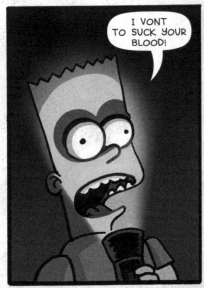

OKAY, LET'S *SPLIT UP* AND LOOK FOR BLANKETS AND FOOD.

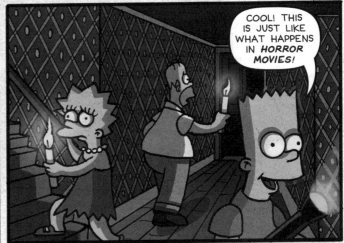

COOL! THIS IS JUST LIKE WHAT HAPPENS IN *HORROR MOVIES!*

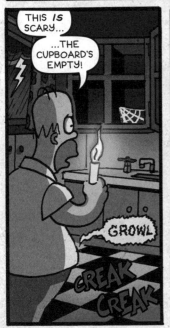

THIS *IS* SCARY...

...THE CUPBOARD'S EMPTY!

GROWL

CREAK CREAK

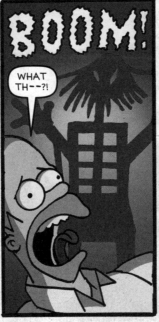

BOOM!

WHAT TH--?!

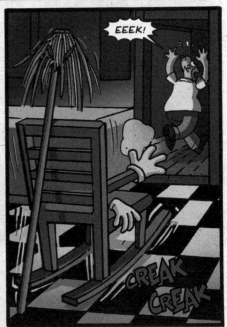

EEEK!

CREAK CREAK

IT SEEMS ABANDONED, BUT AT LEAST THE LIGHTS WORK.
CLICK
HOW WONDERFULLY GOTHIC!
WHOA, MOMMA!
I BET THIS PLACE WOULD BE CREEPY IN THE DARK!
BOOM
D'OH.
I'M GLAD I'M PREPARED FOR EMERGENCIES.
DIBS ON THE FLASHLIGHT!
GOOD THINKING, MOM!

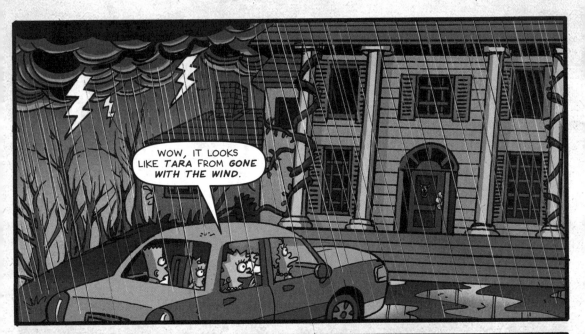

WOW, IT LOOKS LIKE *TARA* FROM *GONE WITH THE WIND.*

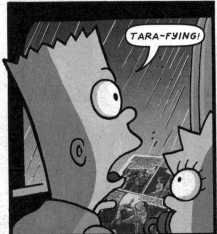

TARA-FYING!

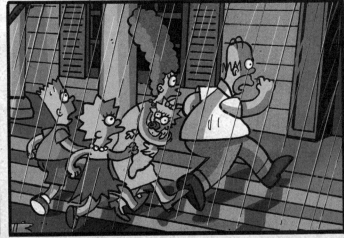

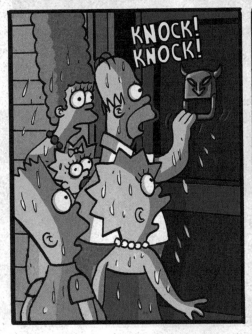

KNOCK! KNOCK!

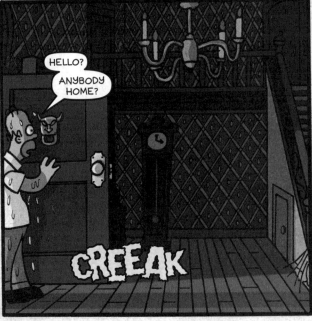

HELLO? ANYBODY HOME?

CREEAK

DID YOU KNOW THAT DURING THE CIVIL WAR--?
BO-RING. ARE WE THERE YET?
HORRIFIC
CHUG!
CHUG!
CHUG!
HOMER, WHEN WAS THE LAST TIME YOU GOT GAS?
BETWEEN "HOTEL CALIFORNIA" AND "HEARTBREAK HOTEL."
WHY?
EMPTY?! *D'OH!*
KA-RACK!
THERE'S A HOUSE. LET'S PULL OVER AND ASK DIRECTIONS.
CHUG!
CHUG!
CHUG!

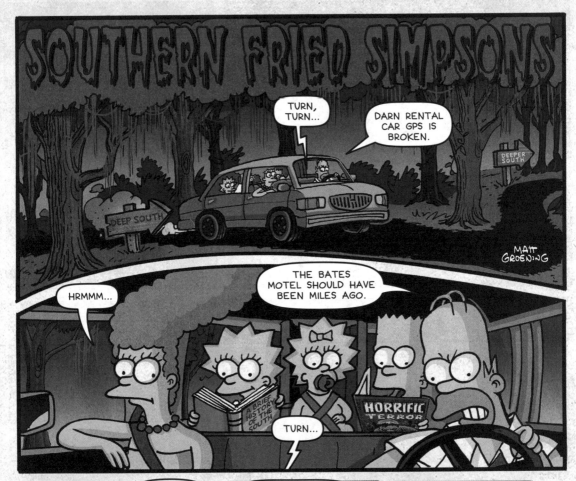

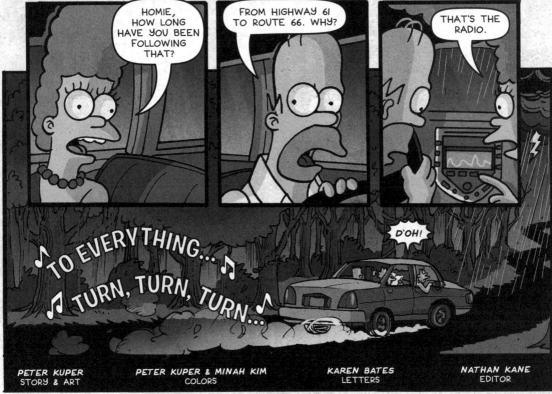

PETER KUPER
STORY & ART

PETER KUPER & MINAH KIM
COLORS

KAREN BATES
LETTERS

NATHAN KANE
EDITOR

MAGGIE'S CRIB

by ARAGONÉS

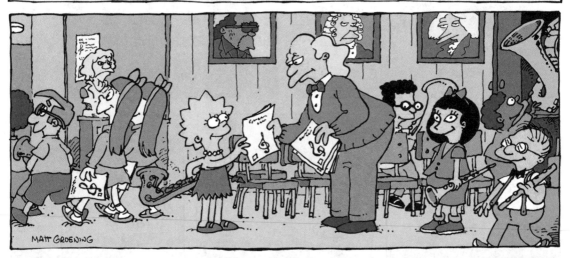

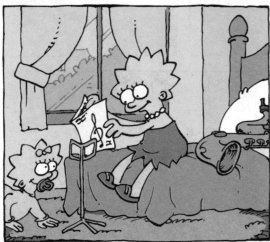

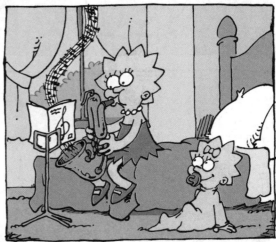

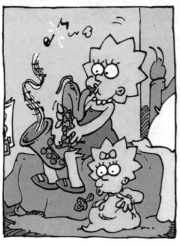

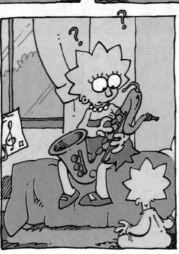

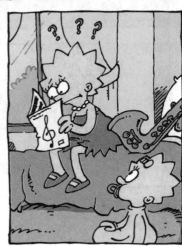

SERGIO ARAGONÉS
STORY & ART

NATHAN HAMILL
COLORS

BILL MORRISON
EDITOR

COME ON, PARTNER! LET'S GO FIND SOME TROUBLE!
DOES TROUBLE LOOK LIKE A SQUIRREL?
BECAUSE THEN I FOUND IT!
WHAT DO WE DO ABOUT THE DONUT BOMB, CHIEF? DESTROY THE BOX?
HE SAID IT WAS ONLY ONE OF THE TWELVE DONUTS. I'M NOT A GAMBLING MAN, BUT I LIKE THOSE ODDS!
KA-SPLORCH!
WHAT'S THAT NOISE?
EYES FORWARD, PARTNER! COOL COPS DON'T LOOK BACK AT EXPLOSIONS!
SPLURCH!
SPLURT!
SPLOIT!
COP OUT!

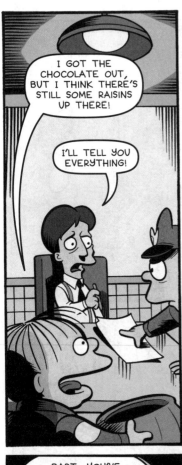

I GOT THE CHOCOLATE OUT, BUT I THINK THERE'S STILL SOME RAISINS UP THERE!

I'LL TELL YOU EVERYTHING!

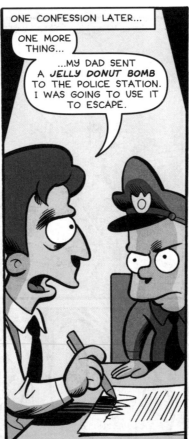

ONE CONFESSION LATER...

ONE MORE THING...

...MY DAD SENT A *JELLY DONUT BOMB* TO THE POLICE STATION. I WAS GOING TO USE IT TO ESCAPE.

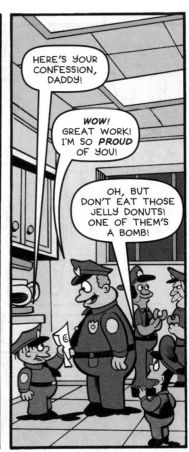

HERE'S YOUR CONFESSION, DADDY!

WOW! GREAT WORK! I'M SO *PROUD* OF YOU!

OH, BUT DON'T EAT THOSE JELLY DONUTS! ONE OF THEM'S A BOMB!

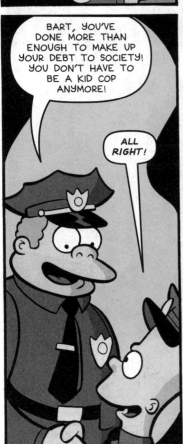

BART, YOU'VE DONE MORE THAN ENOUGH TO MAKE UP YOUR DEBT TO SOCIETY! YOU DON'T HAVE TO BE A KID COP ANYMORE!

ALL RIGHT!

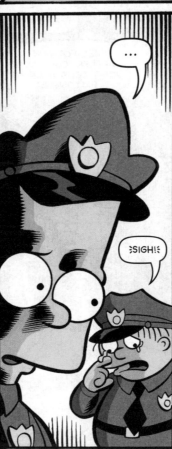

...

:SIGH!:

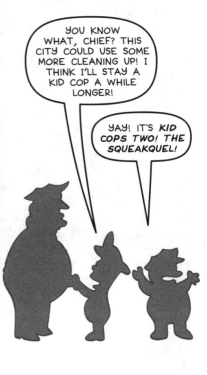

YOU KNOW WHAT, CHIEF? THIS CITY COULD USE SOME MORE CLEANING UP! I THINK I'LL STAY A KID COP A WHILE LONGER!

YAY! IT'S *KID COPS TWO! THE SQUEAKQUEL!*

WHAT? NO!
THEN I GUESS YOU HAVEN'T SEEN EVERYTHING!
HUH? WHAT'S WRONG WITH YOU?
NEVER MIND! JUST CONFESS TO STEALING THAT HALLOWEEN CANDY!
AND IF I DON'T...?
AAAAAH!
I'M STUCK!
WAIT...ARE YOU SAYING YOU'RE GOING TO DO THAT TO ME? I'M CONFUSED.
HOW MANY MINI CHOCOLATE BARS DO YOU THINK I HAVE UP MY NOSE RIGHT NOW?
HE'S TOO SMART FOR US, RALPH. JUST GIVE HIM BACK HIS CHOCOLATE BARS!
NO! NO! I DON'T WANT THEM! KEEP THAT GUY AWAY FROM ME! HE'S CRAZY!

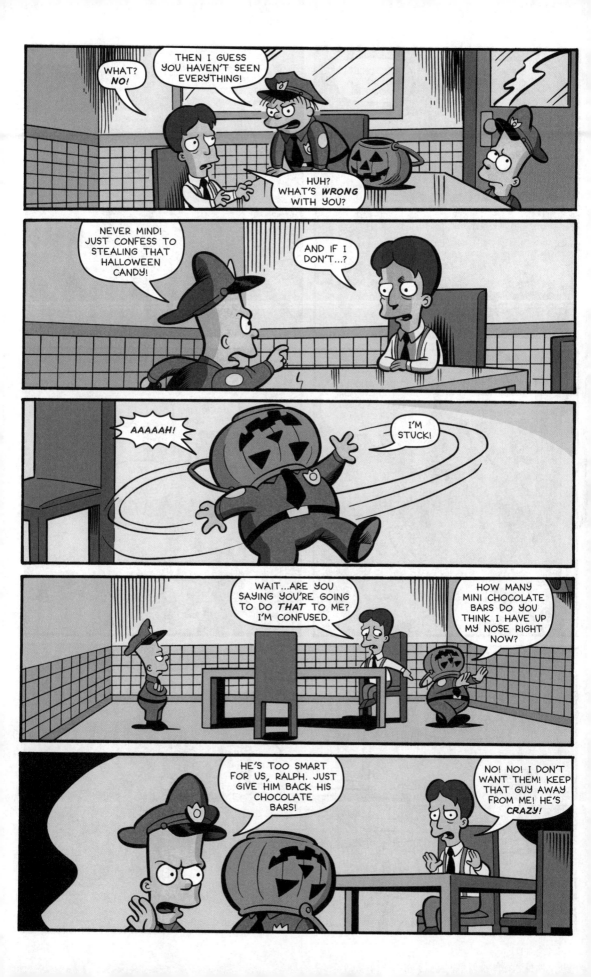

I PLAY BY MY OWN RULES IN SCRABBLE BECAUSE I CAN'T REMEMBER THE REAL ONES.
WHOEVER EATS THE MOST VOWELS WINS!
HEY, CHIEF! WE GOT A PROBLEM!
WHAT IS IT, LOU?
WE GOT FAT TONY'S SON IN THE INTERROGATION ROOM.
WE KNOW HE'S BEEN STEALING HALLOWEEN CANDY FROM YOUNGER KIDS, BUT WE CAN'T GET HIM TO CONFESS.
YEAH! HE'S A HARDER NUT TO CRACK THAN OLD PEANUT BRITTLE!
EDDIE AND I ARE BACHELORS. WE HAVE NO IDEA HOW TO TALK TO KIDS.
YOU'RE BACK ON THE JOB!
I FELL OFF THE CHAIR!
KID COPS? NOW I'VE SEEN EVERYTHING!
OH YEAH?
HAVE YOU EVER SEEN A FLYING PUPPY SNEEZE RAINBOWS?

HEY! WHY ARE YOU RIDING GIRLS' BIKES?
WE ARE?!!!
AAAAH! JUMP OFF!
TUMBLE!
TUMBLE!
SCREEE!
MOAN! WHERE ARE WE?
YOU'RE A LONG WAY FROM HOME, SPRINGFIELDERS!
LET'S GET 'EM!
LET'S GET THESE BIKES BACK TO SHERRI AND TERRI!
WHY WERE YOU PURRING WHEN YOU WERE ASLEEP?
I DREAMED I WAS A KITTY COP!
WANTED
YEAH, YOU SAVED THE BIKES, BUT THERE WAS TEN THOUSAND DOLLARS IN PROPERTY DAMAGE AT THE MALL!
WHAT MAKES YOU THINK YOU CAN PLAY BY YOUR OWN RULES?

COME ON, RALPH! WE'VE GOT TO...
RALPH?!
PURRRRRRR!
POLIZE
POLIZE
RALPH! WAKE UP!
SPRINGFIELD GORGE
ASK ABOUT OUR JAGGED ROCK TOURS
IF I MAKE THIS JUMP, I PROMISE TO GO TO CHURCH EVERY SUNDAY...
LEAP!
YEAH! EVERY SUNDAY THAT FALLS ON FEBRUARY TWENTY-NINTH, THAT IS!
RALPH! WAKE UP!
IS IT MORNING ALREADY?
COME ON, MAN!
WHY IS MY BEDROOM SO WINDY?
ALMOST THERE!
100 FEET TO THE SHELBYVILLE BORDER

HEY, I'M MALL WALKIN' HERE!
WHOA! SLOW DOWN! REMEMBER, HASTE MAKES WASTE!
YEAH, BUT HE WHO HESITATES IS LOST!
LEFT
MOVE IT, DOCTOR DORK!
AAAAH!
HA! IF WE MAKE IT ACROSS THE SHELBYVILLE BORDER, NO SPRINGFIELD COP CAN TOUCH US!
SHELBYVILLE ONE MILE
I KNOW A SHORTCUT JUST PAST THE SPRINGFIELD GORGE!

DON'T LOOK DOWN THAT ALLEY UNLESS YOU'VE GOT A STRONG STOMACH, KID!
PLEASE! ARREST ME AND TAKE ME ANYWHERE WITH A SHOWER!
THE NEXT DAY...
WOW! WE'VE GOT REAL POLICE BIKES!
YOU JUST WROTE "POLICE" ON OUR OWN BIKES, RALPH.
AND YOU SPELLED IT WRONG.
POLIZE
POLIZE
ICE CREAM
HELP! TWO BOYS STOLE OUR BIKES WHEN WE WENT INSIDE TO BUY ICE CREAM!
PLEASE BE LITTLE KIDS, PLEASE BE LITTLE KIDS...
D'OH!
HA! LET'S RIDE THESE UNTIL WE GET BORED AND THEN SMASH 'EM!
MAYBE WE SHOULD JUST...
STOP IN THE NAME OF KID COPS!
POLIZE
POLIZE
RINGFIELD MALL
LET'S DITCH THOSE LOSERS IN THE MALL!

YOU'RE UNDER ARREST FOR STEALING!
MIGHT AS WELL ADD POLICE BRUTALITY TO THE CHARGES!
I NEED SOMETHING TO FIGHT WITH!
PLEASE HAVE A SPORK INSIDE, FAST FOOD BAG!
NERTZ! JUST SALT AND PEPPER PACKS.
HA! ARE YOU GONNA PEPPER SPRAY ME, POLICE DUDE?
SURE, WHY NOT?
THAT DOES IT! HERE COMES THE SMACKDOWN!
FWOOSH!
AAAAH! AAAAH!
AAGH! GROSS! I SURRENDER!
HE LOOKS LIKE A GREEN SNOWMAN!
BLECCH!

PLEASE DON'T TAKE MY ALLOWANCE!
I'M A BULLY. I TAKE DORKS' MONEY. IT'S THE CIRCLE OF LIFE, DUDE!
STOP IN THE NAME OF KID COPS!
QUIET! HE MIGHT HEAR YOU!
OH NO! COPS!
DEAD END
HE RAN DOWN THAT ALLEY!
LET HIM!
REMEMBER, IF RALPHIE GETS HURT IN ANY WAY, YOU'RE OFF TO JUVIE!
YOU DIDN'T SAY THAT BEFORE!
I FORGOT. THAT'S WHY I'M SAYING IT IN YOUR THOUGHTS NOW!
SIGH! WAIT UP, RALPH!
I'VE GOT HIM CORNERED, PARTNER!
IT'S JUST YOU TWO?
HA!
DEAD END

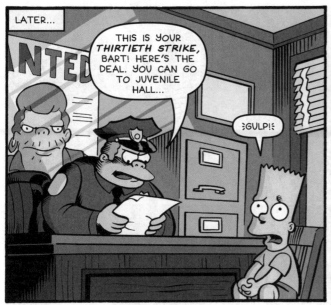

LATER...

THIS IS YOUR *THIRTIETH STRIKE*, BART! HERE'S THE DEAL. YOU CAN GO TO JUVENILE HALL...

¦GULP!¦

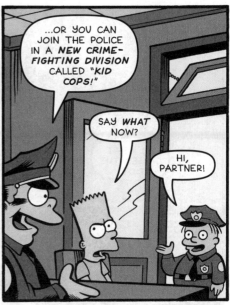

...OR YOU CAN JOIN THE POLICE IN A *NEW CRIME-FIGHTING DIVISION* CALLED "*KID COPS!*"

SAY *WHAT* NOW?

HI, PARTNER!

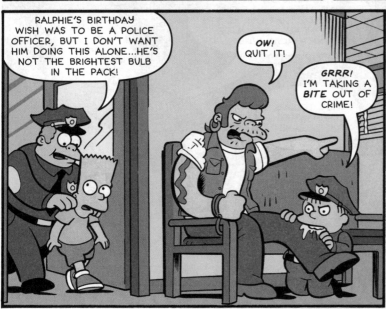

RALPHIE'S BIRTHDAY WISH WAS TO BE A POLICE OFFICER, BUT I DON'T WANT HIM DOING THIS ALONE...HE'S NOT THE BRIGHTEST BULB IN THE PACK!

OW! QUIT IT!

GRRR! I'M TAKING A *BITE* OUT OF CRIME!

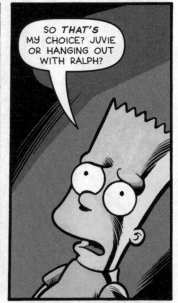

SO *THAT'S* MY CHOICE? JUVIE OR HANGING OUT WITH RALPH?

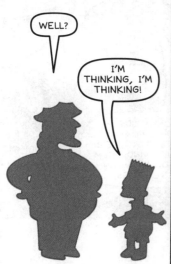

WELL?

I'M THINKING, I'M THINKING!

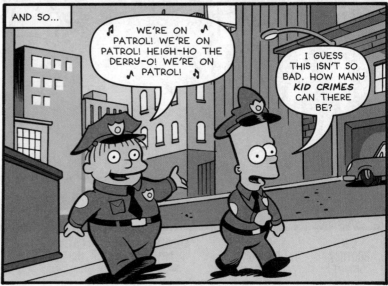

AND SO...

♪ WE'RE ON ♪ PATROL! WE'RE ON PATROL! HEIGH-HO THE DERRY-O! WE'RE ON ♪ PATROL! ♪

I GUESS THIS ISN'T SO BAD. HOW MANY *KID CRIMES* CAN THERE BE?

GOOD COP, BART COP!

SO WHAT CAUSED THE RIOT?
THIS PUNK CONVINCED A BIRTHDAY PARTY OF FIVE-YEAR-OLDS THAT OUR KRUSTY KIDS' MEALS WERE MADE WITH *REAL KIDS!*
I WAS JUST TELLING THEM WHAT THE INTERNET TOLD ME.
THE ONLY KIDS WE USE ARE *GOATS*... AND THAT'S JUST THEIR *HORNS!* WE GRIND THEM UP AS *SEASONING* IN THE CURLY FRIES!
MATT GROENING

IAN BOOTHBY SCRIPT | **JOHN DELANEY** PENCILS | **ANDREW PEPOY** INKS | **NATHAN HAMILL** COLORS | **KAREN BATES** LETTERS | **NATHAN KANE** EDITOR

SHALL WE, M'LADY?
BETTER LUCK NEXT TIME, OLD SPORTS!
SIMPSON?
YEAH?
WE SPEAK OF THIS NEVER.
WOW. SHE DIDN'T PICK ANY OF US. I CAN'T BELIEVE IT.
BUT AT LEAST JANET IS FEELING COMFORTABLE AT HER NEW SCHOOL. ISN'T THAT WHAT THIS WHOLE WAGER WAS ABOUT?
CRAM IT, VAN HOUTEN!
YOU JUST DON'T KNOW ANYTHING ABOUT GIRLS.
THE END

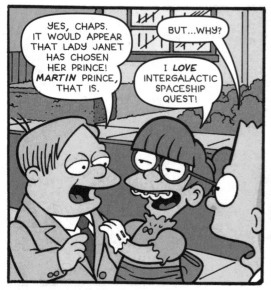

YES, CHAPS. IT WOULD APPEAR THAT LADY JANET HAS CHOSEN HER PRINCE! *MARTIN* PRINCE, THAT IS.

BUT...WHY?

I *LOVE* INTERGALACTIC SPACESHIP QUEST!

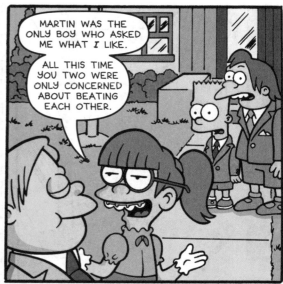

MARTIN WAS THE ONLY BOY WHO ASKED ME WHAT *I* LIKE.

ALL THIS TIME YOU TWO WERE ONLY CONCERNED ABOUT BEATING EACH OTHER.

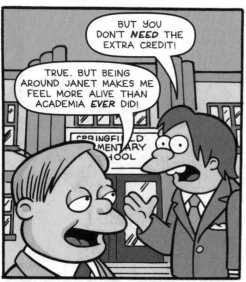

BUT YOU DON'T *NEED* THE EXTRA CREDIT!

TRUE. BUT BEING AROUND JANET MAKES ME FEEL MORE ALIVE THAN ACADEMIA *EVER* DID!

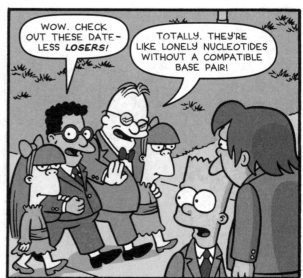

WOW. CHECK OUT THESE DATE-LESS *LOSERS*!

TOTALLY. THEY'RE LIKE LONELY NUCLEOTIDES WITHOUT A COMPATIBLE BASE PAIR!

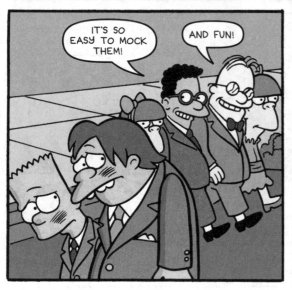

IT'S SO EASY TO MOCK THEM!

AND FUN!

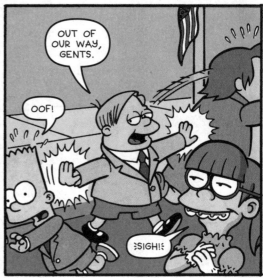

OUT OF OUR WAY, GENTS.

OOF!

:SIGH!:

OKAY, JANET. WHICH ONE OF US IS IT GOING TO BE? BUT REMEMBER, I OFFER AN ENDLESS SUPPLY OF PRINCIPAL SKINNER JOKES!
AND WHAT I LACK IN REFINEMENT, I MORE THAN MAKE UP FOR WITH AN OCEAN OF UNTAPPED EMOTION! ONLY *YOU* CAN FIX ME!
HMMM...I'VE GOT A LOT TO THINK ABOUT. I'LL MAKE MY DECISION AT THE DANCE.
NOT EVEN A HINT?
I'M GOING TO PICK THE *COOLEST* BOY IN SCHOOL. SEE YOU THERE!
THE NIGHT OF THE BOX SOCIAL...
NO HARD FEELINGS, NELSON. BUT EVERYONE KNOWS THAT *I'M* THE COOLEST.
SIMPSON, YOUR DELUSIONS ARE ADMIRABLE, BUT THEY'RE GOING TO EARN YOU A POUNDING.
ARBOR DAY BOX SOCIAL
TREE-MENDOUS FUN
GUYS, I'VE MADE MY CHOICE...
WHAT?!?
THAT'S *IMPOSSIBLE!*

THE NEXT DAY...

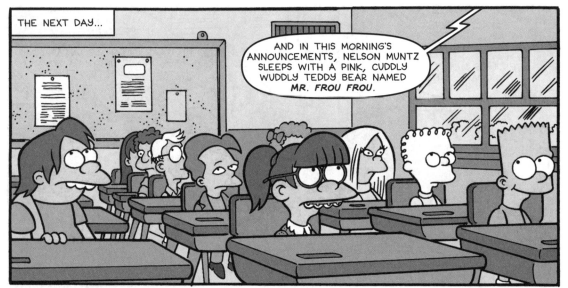

AND IN THIS MORNING'S ANNOUNCEMENTS, NELSON MUNTZ SLEEPS WITH A PINK, CUDDLY WUDDLY TEDDY BEAR NAMED *MR. FROU FROU.*

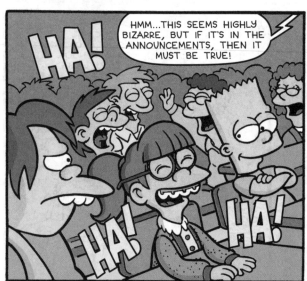

HMM...THIS SEEMS HIGHLY BIZARRE, BUT IF IT'S IN THE ANNOUNCEMENTS, THEN IT MUST BE TRUE!

HA!

HA!

HA!

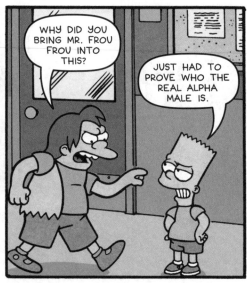

WHY DID YOU BRING MR. FROU FROU INTO THIS?

JUST HAD TO PROVE WHO THE REAL ALPHA MALE IS.

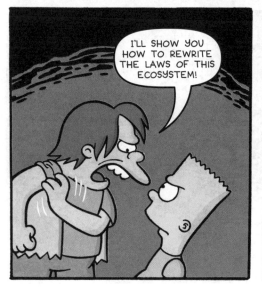

I'LL SHOW YOU HOW TO REWRITE THE LAWS OF THIS ECOSYSTEM!

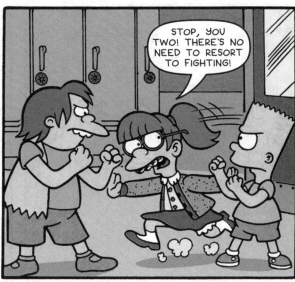

STOP, YOU TWO! THERE'S NO NEED TO RESORT TO FIGHTING!

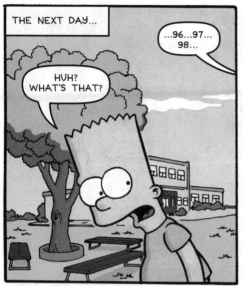

THE NEXT DAY...

...96...97... 98...

HUH? WHAT'S THAT?

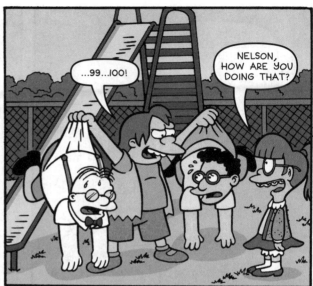

...99...100!

NELSON, HOW ARE YOU DOING THAT?

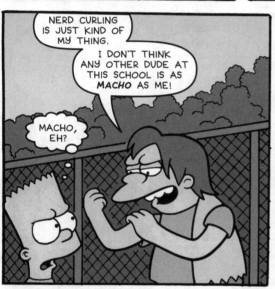

NERD CURLING IS JUST KIND OF MY THING.

I DON'T THINK ANY OTHER DUDE AT THIS SCHOOL IS AS *MACHO* AS ME!

MACHO, EH?

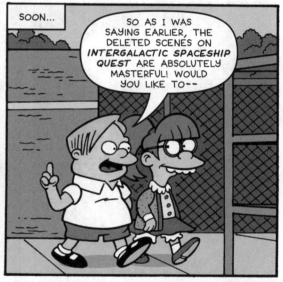

SOON...

SO AS I WAS SAYING EARLIER, THE DELETED SCENES ON *INTERGALACTIC SPACESHIP QUEST* ARE ABSOLUTELY MASTERFUL! WOULD YOU LIKE TO--

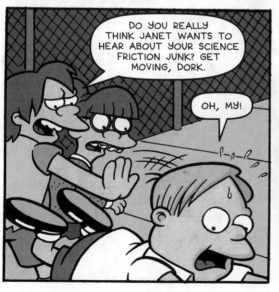

DO YOU REALLY THINK JANET WANTS TO HEAR ABOUT YOUR SCIENCE FRICTION JUNK? GET MOVING, DORK.

OH, MY!

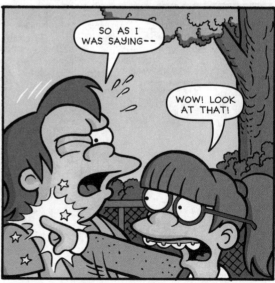

SO AS I WAS SAYING--

WOW! LOOK AT THAT!

BECAUSE THERE'S SOMEONE ELSE WHO WANTS TO ASK THIS LITTLE LADY OUT.
OH MY!
NELSON?!?
DO YOU LIKE MOTORCYCLES? 'CAUSE MY MOM'S BOYFRIEND HAS A HARLEY AND LEAVES THE KEYS ON THE DRESSER.
COOL!
WOW. I CAN'T BELIEVE I'VE GOT TWO SUITORS! WHAT A GREAT SCHOOL THIS IS!
HEY, MAN! WHAT ARE YOU DOING?
YOU THINK YOU'RE THE ONLY ONE WHO NEEDS EXTRA CREDIT? I MIGHT FINALLY GET OUT OF THE FOURTH GRADE!
YOU REALIZE, OF COURSE, THAT THIS MEANS WAR.
GAME ON, DINGUS.
HEY, JANET! CHECK OUT MY BIG BOY SHOES. NO VELCRO! PRETTY BOSS, RIGHT?
ERRR...

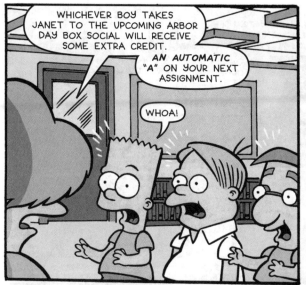

WHICHEVER BOY TAKES JANET TO THE UPCOMING ARBOR DAY BOX SOCIAL WILL RECEIVE SOME EXTRA CREDIT.

AN AUTOMATIC "A" ON YOUR NEXT ASSIGNMENT.

WHOA!

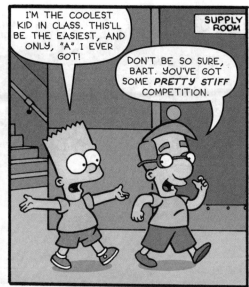

SUPPLY ROOM

I'M THE COOLEST KID IN CLASS. THIS'LL BE THE EASIEST, AND ONLY, "A" I EVER GOT!

DON'T BE SO SURE, BART. YOU'VE GOT SOME PRETTY STIFF COMPETITION.

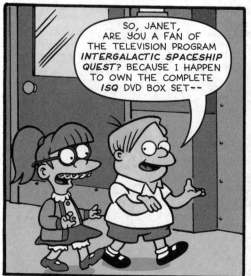

SO, JANET, ARE YOU A FAN OF THE TELEVISION PROGRAM INTERGALACTIC SPACESHIP QUEST? BECAUSE I HAPPEN TO OWN THE COMPLETE ISQ DVD BOX SET--

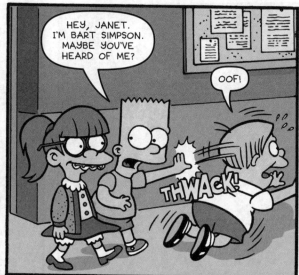

HEY, JANET. I'M BART SIMPSON. MAYBE YOU'VE HEARD OF ME?

OOF!

THWACK!

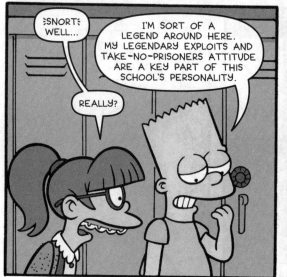

:SNORT: WELL...

I'M SORT OF A LEGEND AROUND HERE. MY LEGENDARY EXPLOITS AND TAKE-NO-PRISONERS ATTITUDE ARE A KEY PART OF THIS SCHOOL'S PERSONALITY.

REALLY?

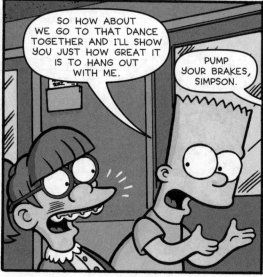

SO HOW ABOUT WE GO TO THAT DANCE TOGETHER AND I'LL SHOW YOU JUST HOW GREAT IT IS TO HANG OUT WITH ME.

PUMP YOUR BRAKES, SIMPSON.

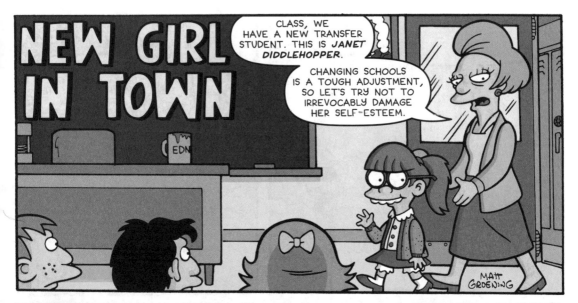

NEW GIRL IN TOWN

CLASS, WE HAVE A NEW TRANSFER STUDENT. THIS IS *JANET DIDDLEHOPPER*.

CHANGING SCHOOLS IS A TOUGH ADJUSTMENT, SO LET'S TRY NOT TO IRREVOCABLY DAMAGE HER SELF-ESTEEM.

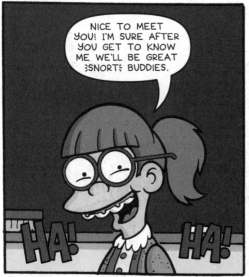

NICE TO MEET YOU! I'M SURE AFTER YOU GET TO KNOW ME WE'LL BE GREAT ¿SNORT¿ BUDDIES.

HA! HA!

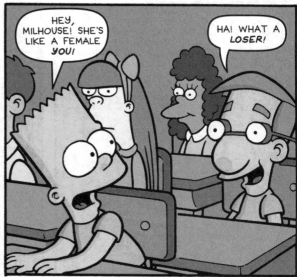

HEY, MILHOUSE! SHE'S LIKE A FEMALE *YOU!*

HA! WHAT A *LOSER!*

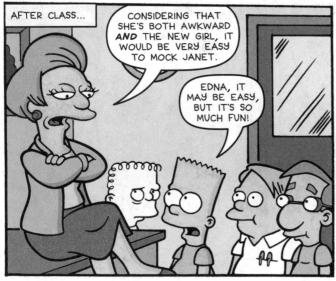

AFTER CLASS...

CONSIDERING THAT SHE'S BOTH AWKWARD *AND* THE NEW GIRL, IT WOULD BE VERY EASY TO MOCK JANET.

EDNA, IT MAY BE EASY, BUT IT'S SO MUCH FUN!

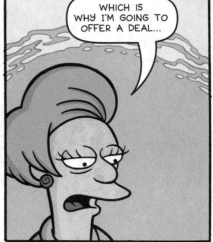

WHICH IS WHY I'M GOING TO OFFER A DEAL...

MAX DAVISON
STORY

PHIL ORTIZ
PENCILS

MIKE DECARLO
INKS

NATHAN HAMILL
COLORS

KAREN BATES
LETTERS

NATHAN KANE
EDITOR

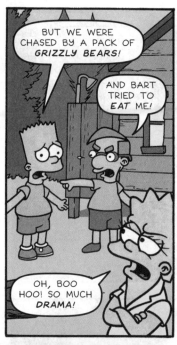

BUT WE WERE CHASED BY A PACK OF *GRIZZLY BEARS!*

AND BART TRIED TO *EAT* ME!

OH, BOO HOO! SO MUCH *DRAMA!*

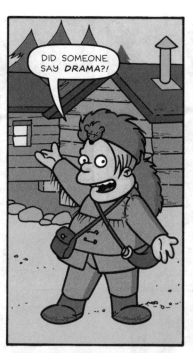

DID SOMEONE SAY *DRAMA?!*

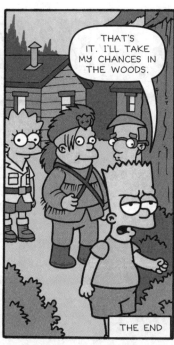

THAT'S IT. I'LL TAKE MY CHANCES IN THE WOODS.

THE END

SPECIAL BONUS!

HERE'S A BIRD'S-EYE VIEW OF BART AND MILHOUSE'S GREAT OUTDOOR ADVENTURE. FOLLOW THEIR TRAIL AND TRY TO DECODE THE SECRET MESSAGE!*

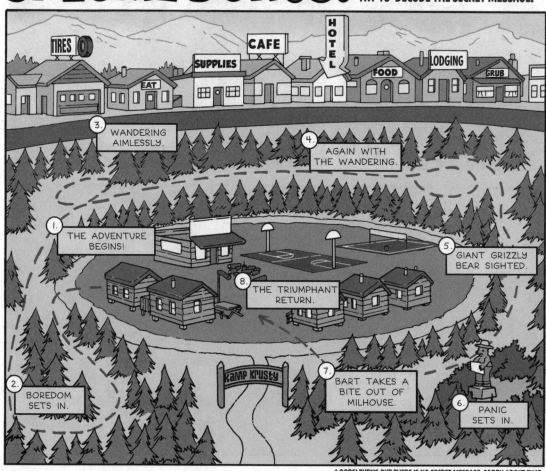

TIRES

SUPPLIES

CAFE

EAT

HOTEL

FOOD

LODGING

GRUB

3. WANDERING AIMLESSLY.

4. AGAIN WITH THE WANDERING.

1. THE ADVENTURE BEGINS!

5. GIANT GRIZZLY BEAR SIGHTED.

8. THE TRIUMPHANT RETURN.

KAMP KRUSTY

7. BART TAKES A BITE OUT OF MILHOUSE.

2. BOREDOM SETS IN.

6. PANIC SETS IN.

* OOPS! TURNS OUT THERE IS NO SECRET MESSAGE. SORRY ABOUT THAT.

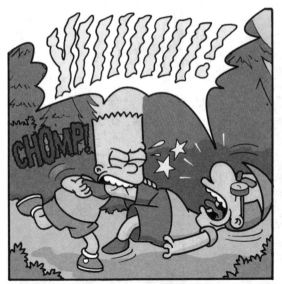

YIIIIIIIII!!

CHOMP!

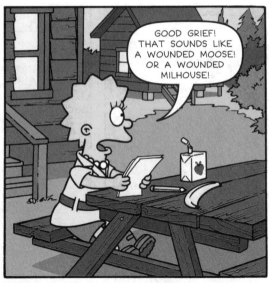

GOOD GRIEF! THAT SOUNDS LIKE A WOUNDED MOOSE! OR A WOUNDED MILHOUSE!

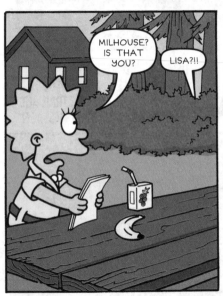

MILHOUSE? IS THAT YOU?

LISA?!!

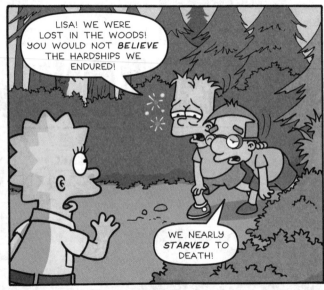

LISA! WE WERE LOST IN THE WOODS! YOU WOULD NOT *BELIEVE* THE HARDSHIPS WE ENDURED!

WE NEARLY *STARVED* TO DEATH!

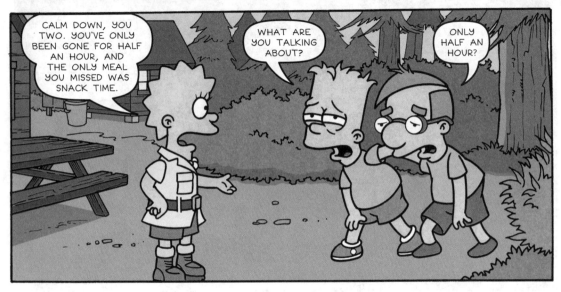

CALM DOWN, YOU TWO. YOU'VE ONLY BEEN GONE FOR HALF AN HOUR, AND THE ONLY MEAL YOU MISSED WAS SNACK TIME.

WHAT ARE YOU TALKING ABOUT?

ONLY HALF AN HOUR?

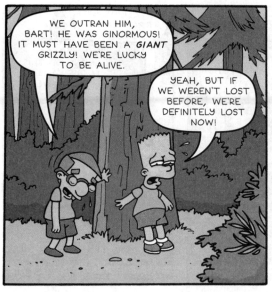

WE OUTRAN HIM, BART! HE WAS GINORMOUS! IT MUST HAVE BEEN A *GIANT* GRIZZLY! WE'RE LUCKY TO BE ALIVE.

YEAH, BUT IF WE WEREN'T LOST BEFORE, WE'RE DEFINITELY LOST NOW!

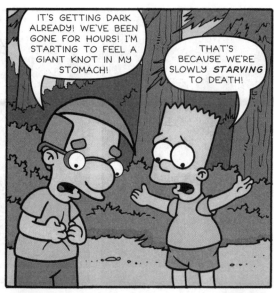

IT'S GETTING DARK ALREADY! WE'VE BEEN GONE FOR HOURS! I'M STARTING TO FEEL A GIANT KNOT IN MY STOMACH!

THAT'S BECAUSE WE'RE SLOWLY *STARVING* TO DEATH!

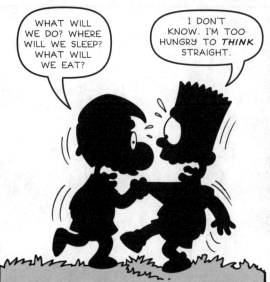

WHAT WILL WE DO? WHERE WILL WE SLEEP? WHAT WILL WE EAT?

I DON'T KNOW. I'M TOO HUNGRY TO *THINK* STRAIGHT.

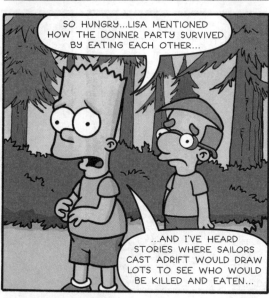

SO HUNGRY...LISA MENTIONED HOW THE DONNER PARTY SURVIVED BY EATING EACH OTHER...

...AND I'VE HEARD STORIES WHERE SAILORS CAST ADRIFT WOULD DRAW LOTS TO SEE WHO WOULD BE KILLED AND EATEN...

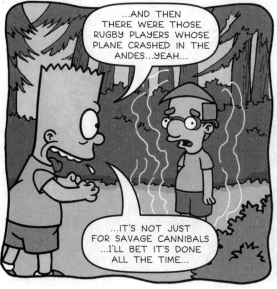

...AND THEN THERE WERE THOSE RUGBY PLAYERS WHOSE PLANE CRASHED IN THE ANDES...YEAH...

...IT'S NOT JUST FOR SAVAGE CANNIBALS ...I'LL BET IT'S DONE ALL THE TIME...

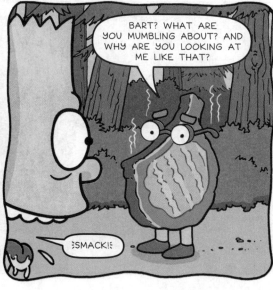

BART? WHAT ARE YOU MUMBLING ABOUT? AND WHY ARE YOU LOOKING AT ME LIKE THAT?

:SMACK!:

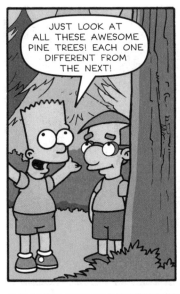

JUST LOOK AT ALL THESE AWESOME PINE TREES! EACH ONE DIFFERENT FROM THE NEXT!

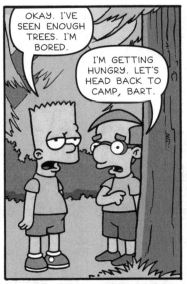

OKAY. I'VE SEEN ENOUGH TREES. I'M BORED.

I'M GETTING HUNGRY. LET'S HEAD BACK TO CAMP, BART.

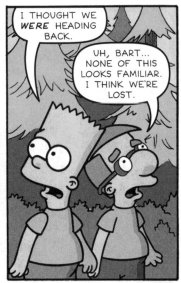

I THOUGHT WE *WERE* HEADING BACK.

UH, BART... NONE OF THIS LOOKS FAMILIAR. I THINK WE'RE LOST.

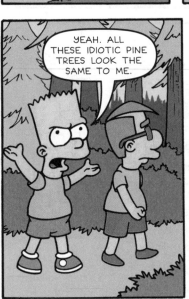

YEAH. ALL THESE IDIOTIC PINE TREES LOOK THE SAME TO ME.

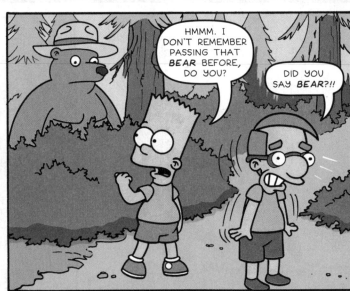

HMMM. I DON'T REMEMBER PASSING THAT *BEAR* BEFORE, DO YOU?

DID YOU SAY *BEAR*?!!

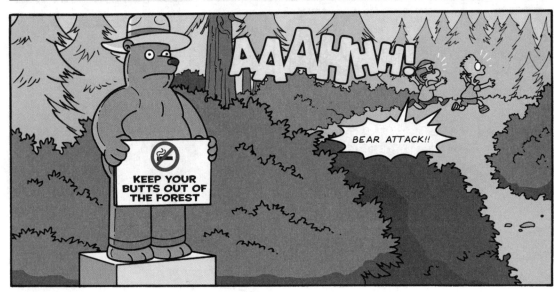

AAAHHH!

BEAR ATTACK!!

KEEP YOUR BUTTS OUT OF THE FOREST

IT SOUNDS FASCINATING, MARTIN! YOU KNOW, THE DONNER PARTY GOT LOST ON THEIR WAY TO CALIFORNIA AND RESORTED TO **CANNIBALISM** IN ORDER TO SURVIVE!
WERE THEY TOO CHEAP TO INSTALL GPS ON THEIR CONESTOGA WAGONS?
GOOD ONE, BART!
DON'T PAY ANY ATTENTION TO THEM, MARTIN. THEY THINK "THE OLD WEST" IS AN ACTOR WHO PLAYED BATMAN ON TV.
GET LOST, BART!
NOW, NOW, LISA. ONE MUST **NEVER** STOOP TO THE LEVEL OF THE PHILISTINES.
C'MON, MILHOUSE. LET'S GET AWAY FROM THESE DORKS AND EXPLORE THE DEEP WOODS.
WELL...LET'S BE SURE TO BE BACK IN TIME FOR LUNCH, OKAY? MY MOM SAYS I'M A REAL **BEAR** WHEN MY BLOOD SUGAR DROPS!
THIS IS WHAT KAMP KRUSTY IS ALL ABOUT, MILHOUSE! NOT WATCHING SOME PRISSY PAGEANT ABOUT A BUNCH OF LOSERS WITH NO SENSE OF DIRECTION.
YEAH. STUPID PIONEERS! THEY MAKE ME SO **ANGRY**!

INTO THE WOODS

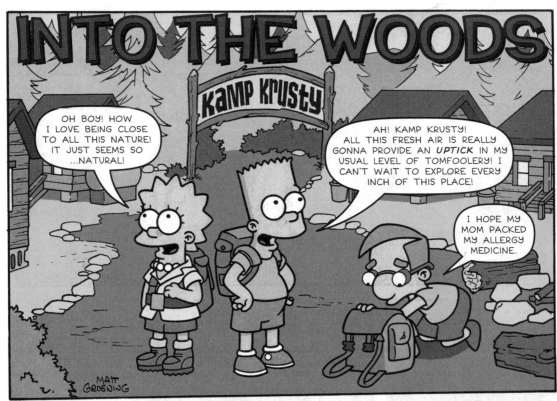

KAMP KRUSTY

OH BOY! HOW I LOVE BEING CLOSE TO ALL THIS NATURE! IT JUST SEEMS SO ...NATURAL!

AH! KAMP KRUSTY! ALL THIS FRESH AIR IS REALLY GONNA PROVIDE AN *UPTICK* IN MY USUAL LEVEL OF TOMFOOLERY! I CAN'T WAIT TO EXPLORE EVERY INCH OF THIS PLACE!

I HOPE MY MOM PACKED MY ALLERGY MEDICINE.

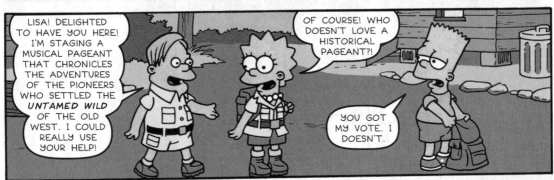

LISA! DELIGHTED TO HAVE YOU HERE! I'M STAGING A MUSICAL PAGEANT THAT CHRONICLES THE ADVENTURES OF THE PIONEERS WHO SETTLED THE *UNTAMED WILD* OF THE OLD WEST. I COULD REALLY USE YOUR HELP!

OF COURSE! WHO DOESN'T LOVE A HISTORICAL PAGEANT?!

YOU GOT MY VOTE. I DOESN'T.

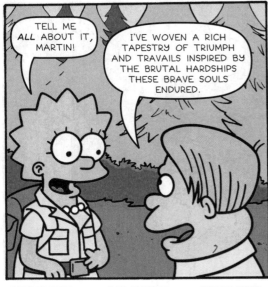

TELL ME *ALL* ABOUT IT, MARTIN!

I'VE WOVEN A RICH TAPESTRY OF TRIUMPH AND TRAVAILS INSPIRED BY THE BRUTAL HARDSHIPS THESE BRAVE SOULS ENDURED.

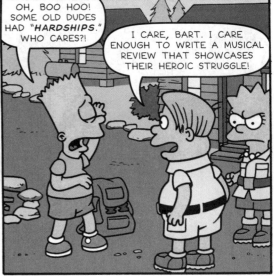

OH, BOO HOO! SOME OLD DUDES HAD "*HARDSHIPS.*" WHO CARES?!

I CARE, BART. I CARE ENOUGH TO WRITE A MUSICAL REVIEW THAT SHOWCASES THEIR HEROIC STRUGGLE!

MARY TRAINOR
SCRIPT

JOHN COSTANZA
PENCILS

PHYLLIS NOVIN
INKS

NATHAN HAMILL
COLORS

KAREN BATES
LETTERS

NATHAN KANE
EDITOR

MAGGIE'S CRIB

by ARAGONÉS

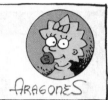

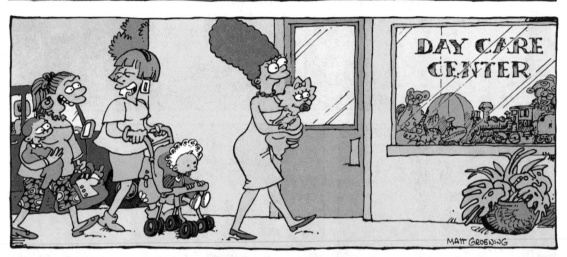

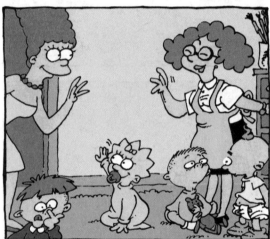

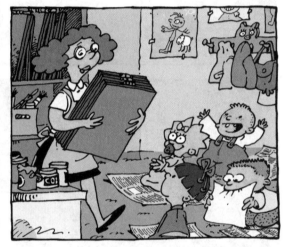

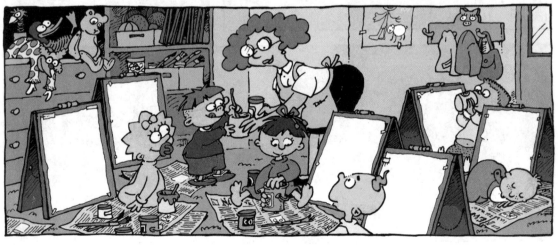

SERGIO ARAGONÉS
STORY & ART

NATHAN HAMILL
COLORS

BILL MORRISON
EDITOR

SMASH! CRASH!
BONK!
ARE THOSE ONE-OF-A-KIND? I'LL TAKE TEN!
GIMME GIMME GIMME!!!!
SHE'S LIKE A YOUNG FRANK LLOYD WRIGHT!
I NEED THAT NOW!
IT IS ABSOLUTELY MASTERFUL!
SIGH!
PURE GENIUS!
THE END

I'VE GOT SOLE, MAN!

BART SIMPSON'S

Believe It or Knot!®

FUN SHOE FACTS FOR THE WHOLE FAMILY

- DURING THE MIDDLE AGES, PEOPLE WORE FRESHLY-BAKED PIES ON THEIR FEET ***TO KEEP WARM!***
- EVERYONE WILL WEAR ***EXACTLY 1575 PAIRS OF SHOES IN*** THEIR LIFETIME. ***NO MORE, NO LESS!***
- GOULASH IS ACTUALLY MADE FROM ***OLD GALOSHES!***
- ***DR. MARTENS*** AND ***DR. SCHOLL*** WERE ROOMMATES IN COLLEGE!
- THE TONGUE OF A SHOE WAS ORIGINALLY MADE OF ***CROCODILE TONGUE!***
- YOUR RIGHT FOOT ***IS STINKIER THAN YOUR LEFT FOOT. IT'S SCIENTIFICALLY PROVEN!***
- SHOES LAST ***LONGER*** WHEN THEY ARE STORED IN A CONTAINER OF ***TUNA FISH!***
- SLAPPING A BEAR WITH A PAIR OF FLIP-FLOPS IS RARELY ***DANGEROUS!***
- IN MANY COUNTRIES, IT'S CONSIDERED RUDE ***TO WEAR PENNY LOAFERS ON TUESDAYS!***

UGH! I'M GIVING THESE "FACTS" THE BOOT!

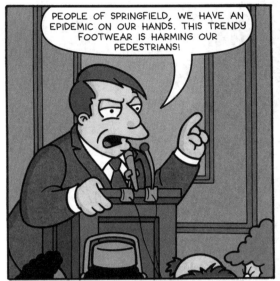

PEOPLE OF SPRINGFIELD, WE HAVE AN EPIDEMIC ON OUR HANDS. THIS TRENDY FOOTWEAR IS HARMING OUR PEDESTRIANS!

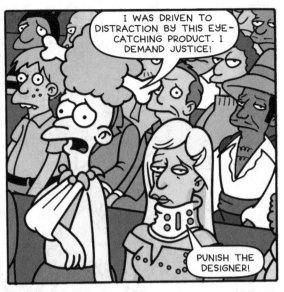

I WAS DRIVEN TO DISTRACTION BY THIS EYE-CATCHING PRODUCT. I DEMAND JUSTICE!

PUNISH THE DESIGNER!

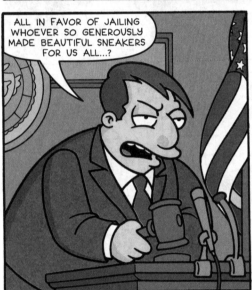

ALL IN FAVOR OF JAILING WHOEVER SO GENEROUSLY MADE BEAUTIFUL SNEAKERS FOR US ALL...?

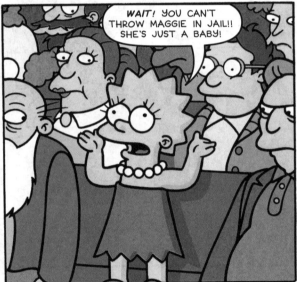

WAIT! YOU CAN'T THROW MAGGIE IN JAIL!! SHE'S JUST A BABY!

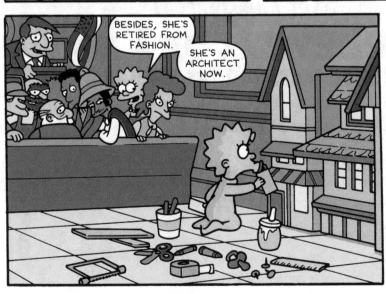

BESIDES, SHE'S RETIRED FROM FASHION.

SHE'S AN ARCHITECT NOW.

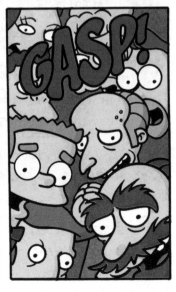

GASP!

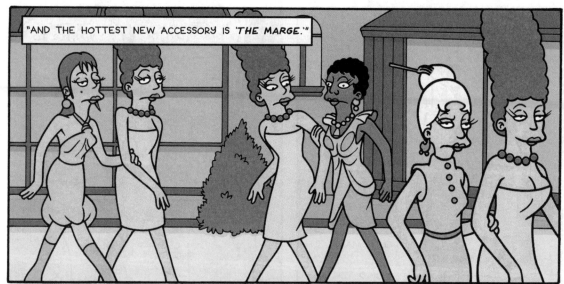

"AND THE HOTTEST NEW ACCESSORY IS *THE MARGE.*"

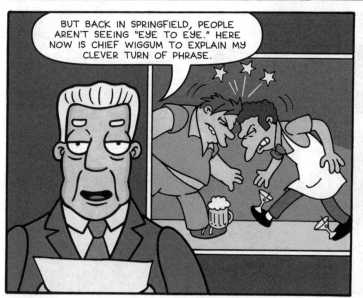

BUT BACK IN SPRINGFIELD, PEOPLE AREN'T SEEING "EYE TO EYE." HERE NOW IS CHIEF WIGGUM TO EXPLAIN MY CLEVER TURN OF PHRASE.

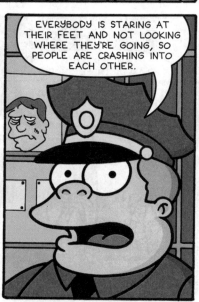

EVERYBODY IS STARING AT THEIR FEET AND NOT LOOKING WHERE THEY'RE GOING, SO PEOPLE ARE CRASHING INTO EACH OTHER.

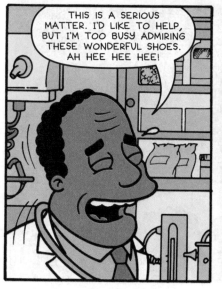

THIS IS A SERIOUS MATTER. I'D LIKE TO HELP, BUT I'M TOO BUSY ADMIRING THESE WONDERFUL SHOES. AH HEE HEE HEE!

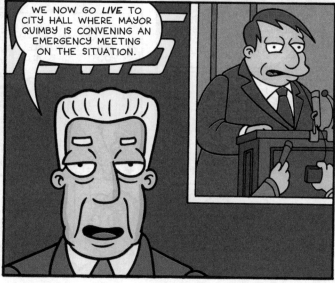

WE NOW GO *LIVE* TO CITY HALL WHERE MAYOR QUIMBY IS CONVENING AN EMERGENCY MEETING ON THE SITUATION.

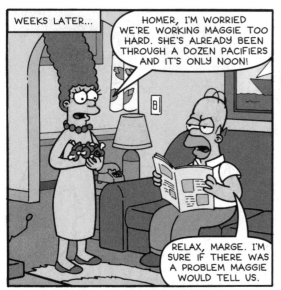

WEEKS LATER...

HOMER, I'M WORRIED WE'RE WORKING MAGGIE TOO HARD. SHE'S ALREADY BEEN THROUGH A DOZEN PACIFIERS AND IT'S ONLY NOON!

RELAX, MARGE. I'M SURE IF THERE WAS A PROBLEM MAGGIE WOULD TELL US.

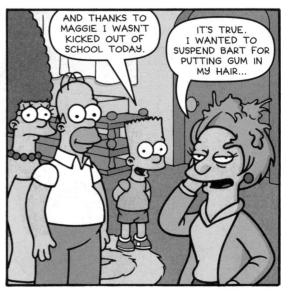

AND THANKS TO MAGGIE I WASN'T KICKED OUT OF SCHOOL TODAY.

IT'S TRUE. I WANTED TO SUSPEND BART FOR PUTTING GUM IN MY HAIR...

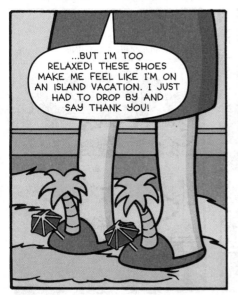

...BUT I'M TOO RELAXED! THESE SHOES MAKE ME FEEL LIKE I'M ON AN ISLAND VACATION. I JUST HAD TO DROP BY AND SAY THANK YOU!

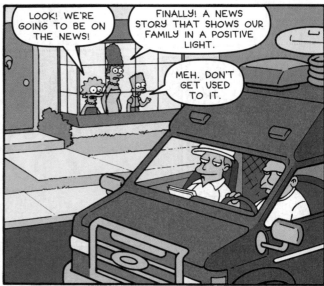

LOOK! WE'RE GOING TO BE ON THE NEWS!

FINALLY! A NEWS STORY THAT SHOWS OUR FAMILY IN A POSITIVE LIGHT.

MEH. DON'T GET USED TO IT.

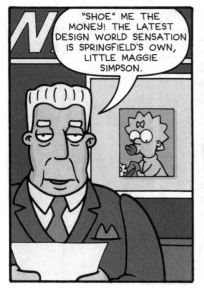

"SHOE" ME THE MONEY! THE LATEST DESIGN WORLD SENSATION IS SPRINGFIELD'S OWN, LITTLE MAGGIE SIMPSON.

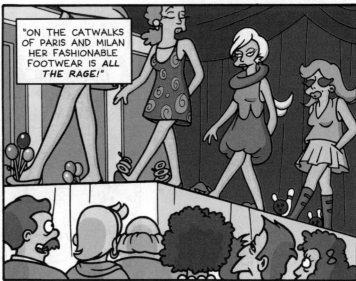

"ON THE CATWALKS OF PARIS AND MILAN HER FASHIONABLE FOOTWEAR IS *ALL THE RAGE!*"

THEN WE'RE GOING TO NEED THESE MEGAPHONES!
GET YOUR SHOES HERE! TREAT YOUR FEET TO A SHOE SENSATION!
YOU WON'T BOO...
...YOU'LL SQUEAL AND COO...
...WHEN YOU SEE THE SHOE...
...DESIGNED BY YOU-KNOW-WHO!
HEY, BOY, WHAT ELSE RHYMES WITH "SHOE?"
MOO, GOO, ZOO, POO...
THESE SOLES ARE GOOD FOR THE SOUL!
BUT WE WILL ANYWAY.
THEY'RE *SMOKIN'*, SO WE DON'T HAVE TO!
I CAN RAMBLE ALL I WANT AND THESE EAR SHOES WILL LISTEN! OF COURSE, IN MY DAY WE CALLED THEM **CLOG BOTTOMS!** AND WE MADE THEM OURSELVES WITH SPIT AND POTATO SKINS! THAT WAS BACK WHEN YOU COULD BUY SOUP FOR A HANDSHAKE AND THE PRESIDENT WAS RIN TIN TIN!
I LOVE-A THAT MY FEET SMELL LIKE **PEPPERONI** AND NOT-A THE STINKY CHEESE!
MY *TRAILER PARK* SHOES IS DOUBLE-WIDE!
MY *FEETS* ARE ASLEEP!

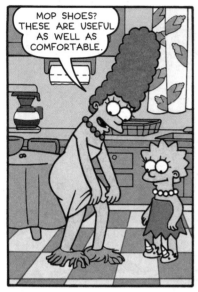

MOP SHOES? THESE ARE USEFUL AS WELL AS COMFORTABLE.

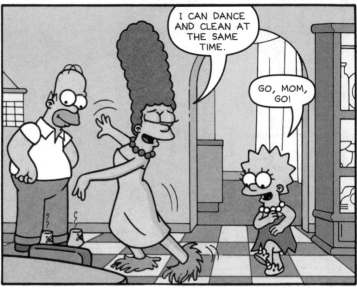

I CAN DANCE AND CLEAN AT THE SAME TIME.

GO, MOM, GO!

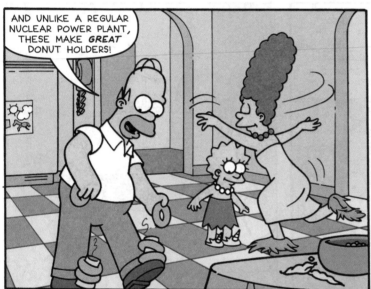

AND UNLIKE A REGULAR NUCLEAR POWER PLANT, THESE MAKE *GREAT* DONUT HOLDERS!

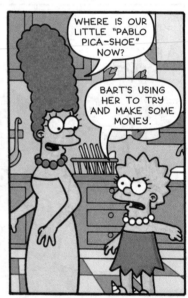

WHERE IS OUR LITTLE "PABLO PICA-SHOE" NOW?

BART'S USING HER TO TRY AND MAKE SOME MONEY.

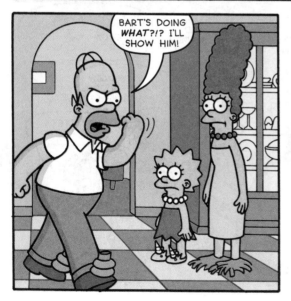

BART'S DOING *WHAT*?!? I'LL SHOW HIM!

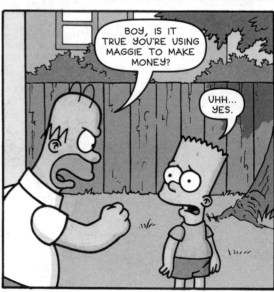

BOY, IS IT TRUE YOU'RE USING MAGGIE TO MAKE MONEY?

UHH... YES.

LET'S TAKE THESE BAD BOYS FOR A SPIN.
DO MINE NEXT!
ZOOM!
THE KIDS ARE AWFULLY QUIET.
SHOULD I GO YELL AT THEM?
DONUT MONTHLY
MOM! DAD! LOOK!
SO MUCH FOR QUIET.
MAGGIE MADE SHOES FOR THE WHOLE FAMILY!
OH MY! IT LOOKS LIKE WE HAVE A COBBLER IN THE FAMILY.
MMM... COBBLER.
SHE MADE UNICORN SHOES FOR ME!
AND POWER PLANT SHOES FOR ME! THEY LOOK GOOD ENOUGH TO ALMOST REGRET DITCHING WORK TODAY.

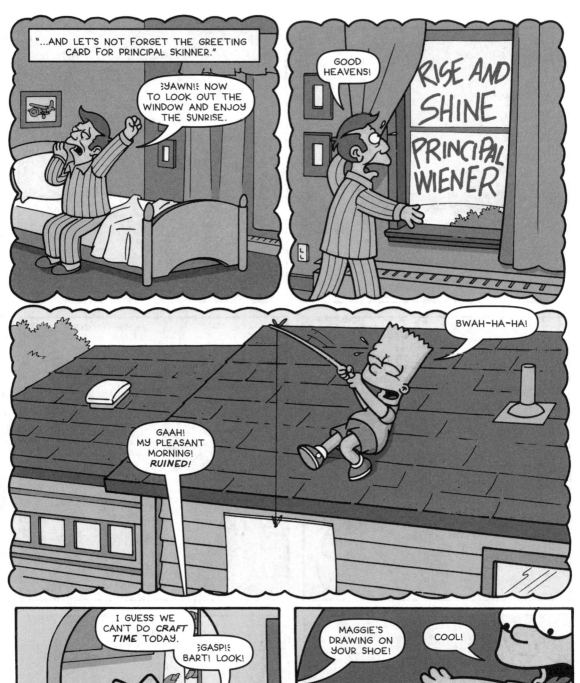

"...AND LET'S NOT FORGET THE GREETING CARD FOR PRINCIPAL SKINNER."

¡YAWN!¡ NOW TO LOOK OUT THE WINDOW AND ENJOY THE SUNRISE.

GOOD HEAVENS!

RISE AND SHINE PRINCIPAL WIENER

BWAH-HA-HA!

GAAH! MY PLEASANT MORNING! *RUINED!*

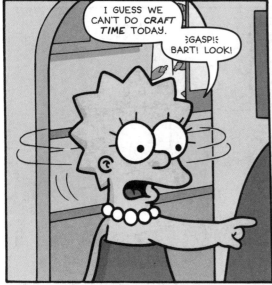

I GUESS WE CAN'T DO *CRAFT TIME* TODAY.

¡GASP!¡ BART! LOOK!

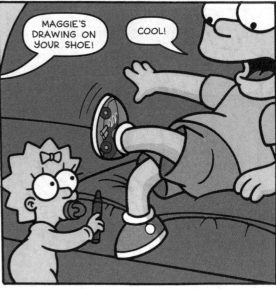

MAGGIE'S DRAWING ON YOUR SHOE!

COOL!

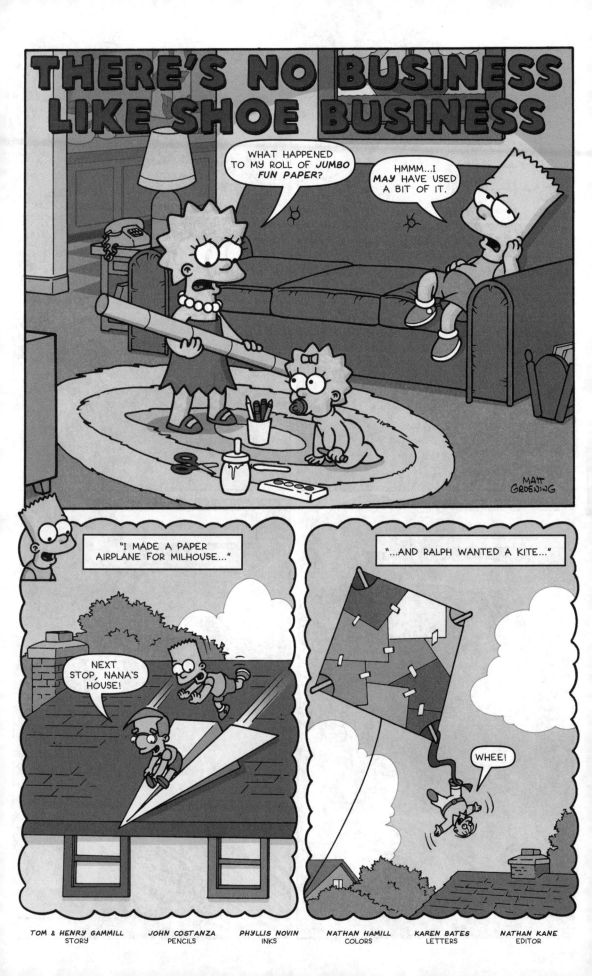

THERE'S NO BUSINESS LIKE SHOE BUSINESS

WHAT HAPPENED TO MY ROLL OF *JUMBO FUN PAPER?*

HMMM...I *MAY* HAVE USED A BIT OF IT.

MATT GROENING

"I MADE A PAPER AIRPLANE FOR MILHOUSE..."

NEXT STOP, NANA'S HOUSE!

"...AND RALPH WANTED A KITE..."

WHEE!

TOM & HENRY GAMMILL
STORY

JOHN COSTANZA
PENCILS

PHYLLIS NOVIN
INKS

NATHAN HAMILL
COLORS

KAREN BATES
LETTERS

NATHAN KANE
EDITOR

...HIS ENEMY, *SIDESHOW BOB*...
HIS REFUSAL TO DIE GNAWS AT MY VERY SOUL!
...THE ALIEN INVADERS, *KANG* AND *KODOS*...
HE SHOULD BE BATHED IN BUTTER, I SAY!
NONSENSE! OLIVE OIL IS BEST!
EEP!
...HIS LOYAL TOADY, *MILHOUSE*...
WHAT'S A TOADY?
...AND BART *HIMSELF*.
TO QUOTE A WISE MAN, "I YAM, WHAT I YAM!"
THE END

THE MANY FACES OF BART

WHAT DO PEOPLE THINK OF SPRINGFIELD'S NUMBER ONE BAD BOY?

ENTER THEIR MINDS TO SEE...

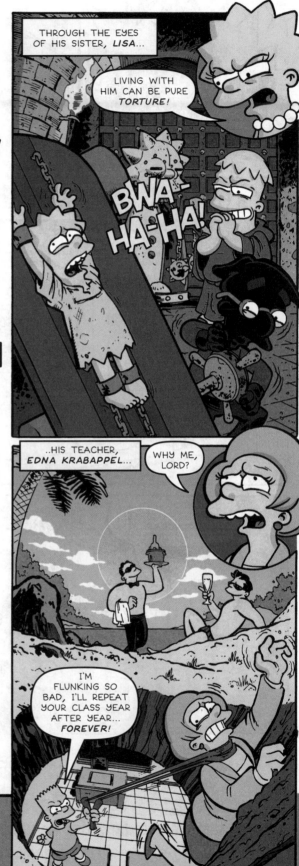

THROUGH THE EYES OF HIS SISTER, *LISA*...

LIVING WITH HIM CAN BE PURE *TORTURE!*

BWA-HA-HA!

..HIS TEACHER, *EDNA KRABAPPEL*...

WHY ME, LORD?

I'M FLUNKING SO BAD, I'LL REPEAT YOUR CLASS YEAR AFTER YEAR... *FOREVER!*

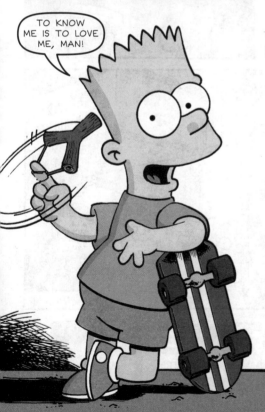

TO KNOW ME IS TO LOVE ME, MAN!

MATT GROENING

DAVID SEIDMAN
SCRIPT

TONE RODRIGUEZ
PENCILS & INKS

NATHAN HAMILL
COLORS

KAREN BATES
LETTERS

NATHAN KANE
EDITOR

CRASH!
OOOOHHHHH. I'M GONNA FEEL THAT TOMORROW FOR SURE.
ITCHY AND SCRATCHY, HERE I COME!
ARE YOU ALL RIGHT, BART?
YOU *BET* I AM! I GOT HERE BEFORE *YOU* DID!
YOU SURE DID!
YOU WERE PASSED OUT IN THAT TREE FOR *TWO HOURS!* THE MOVIE'S *OVER!*
D'OH!
ITCHY AND SCRATCHY 3-D
ITCHY AND SCR
NOW WITH MORE
ALL SHOWS SOLD OUT
THE END

RADIOACTIVE MAN
RADIOACTIVE REPOSITORY VOLUME ONE

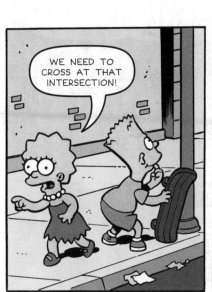

WE NEED TO CROSS AT THAT INTERSECTION!

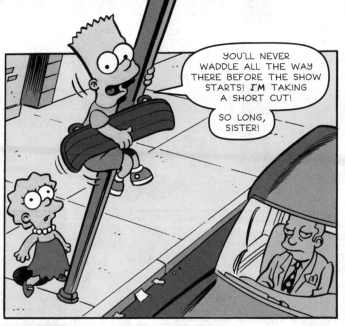

YOU'LL NEVER WADDLE ALL THE WAY THERE BEFORE THE SHOW STARTS! *I'M* TAKING A SHORT CUT!

SO LONG, SISTER!

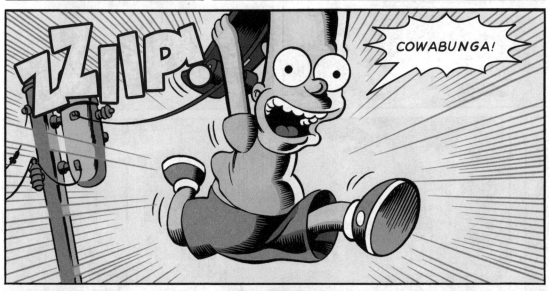

ZZIP!

COWABUNGA!

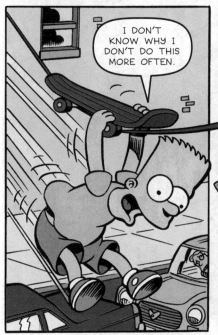

I DON'T KNOW WHY I DON'T DO THIS MORE OFTEN.

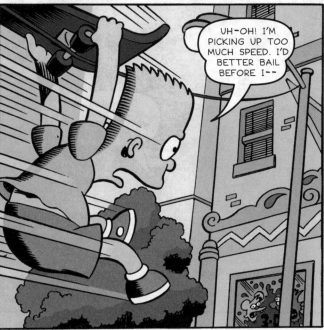

UH-OH! I'M PICKING UP TOO MUCH SPEED. I'D BETTER BAIL BEFORE I--

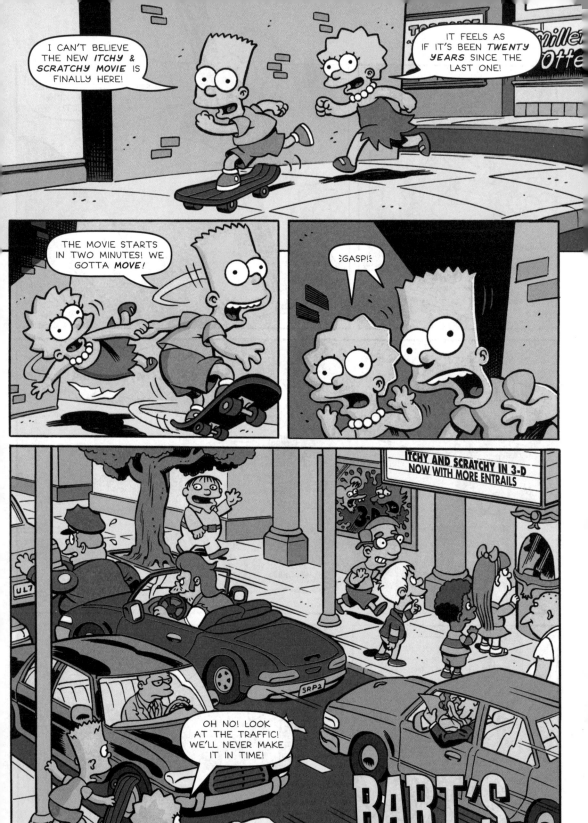

DAVID SEIDMAN
SCRIPT

HILARY BARTA
PENCILS & INKS

NATHAN HAMILL
COLORS

KAREN BATES
LETTERS

NATHAN KANE
EDITOR

AND WHY DIDN'T I LISTEN TO BART?
THAT'S MUSIC TO MY EARS, SIS.
BART! MAGGIE! YOU FOUND ME!
SUCK
SUCK
BUT NOW YOU'LL BE LOST, TOO! THIS MAZE IS IMPOSSIBLE! WE'RE DOOMED!
AU CONTRAIRE, MA SOEUR.
YOU GOTTA THINK OUTSIDE THE LINES SOME-TIMES, LISA.
C'MON. WE CUT A STRAIGHT LINE THROUGH AND WE'LL BE OUT OF HERE IN NO TIME.
BUT CUTTING THROUGH THE STALKS? THAT'S CHEATING! I'M NOT A CHEATER! WHAT ABOUT MY HONOR?!
GR-R-R-OWWWLLLL
HEH, HEH... OH YEAH, RIGHT...
LEAD ON, MACDUFF!
C'MON, I'LL BUY YOU A CORN MUFFIN.
THE END

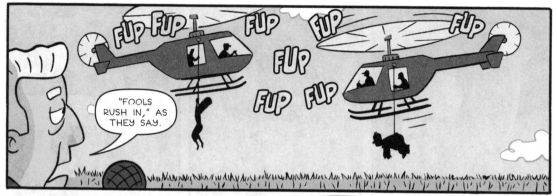

"FOOLS RUSH IN," AS THEY SAY.

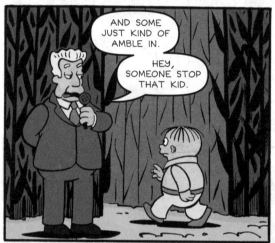

AND SOME JUST KIND OF AMBLE IN.

HEY, SOMEONE STOP THAT KID.

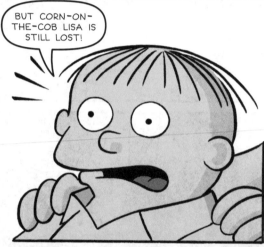

BUT CORN-ON-THE-COB LISA IS STILL LOST!

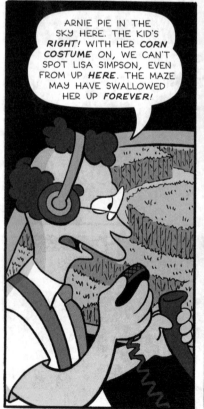

ARNIE PIE IN THE SKY HERE. THE KID'S *RIGHT!* WITH HER *CORN COSTUME* ON, WE CAN'T SPOT LISA SIMPSON, EVEN FROM UP *HERE.* THE MAZE MAY HAVE SWALLOWED HER UP *FOREVER!*

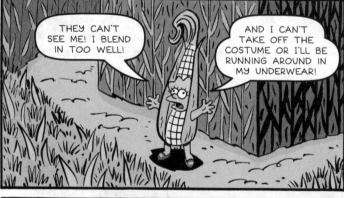

THEY CAN'T SEE ME! I BLEND IN TOO WELL!

AND I CAN'T TAKE OFF THE COSTUME OR I'LL BE RUNNING AROUND IN MY UNDERWEAR!

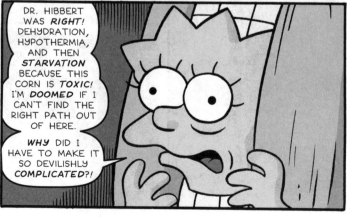

DR. HIBBERT WAS *RIGHT!* DEHYDRATION, HYPOTHERMIA, AND THEN *STARVATION* BECAUSE THIS CORN IS *TOXIC!* I'M *DOOMED* IF I CAN'T FIND THE RIGHT PATH OUT OF HERE.

WHY DID I HAVE TO MAKE IT SO DEVILISHLY *COMPLICATED*?!

I'M COMING, LISA!
WAIT, HOMER, OR YOU'LL GET...
MARGE! HELLLP!
...LOST.
I LOVE YOU, BART.
TAKE CARE OF YOUR LITTLE SISTER.
I'M COMING, HOMIE!
ZING!
TRIUMPH TURNS INTO TRAGEDY AS A LITTLE GIRL IS LOST IN HER OWN MAZE OF MADNESS!
AND NOW HER PARENTS ARE RISKING THEIR OWN LIVES TO SAVE HER! WHEN WILL THIS END?!
HELLLP!
HELLLP!
HELLLP!

I DON'T KNOW WHY *I* HAVE TO DO EVERYTHING AROUND HERE!
AND AFTER A WHILE...
HEY, THIS ISN'T RIGHT.
THERE'S A *ZAG* WHERE THERE SHOULD BE A *ZIG*.
I OUGHT TO BE IN MURPHY'S *SHADES* BY NOW.
BUT SOMEHOW THIS FEELS MORE LIKE HIS *BLEEDING GUMS*.
EEEW.
IF SO, THERE SHOULD BE A POOL OF FAKE BLOOD HERE, BUT...
UH-OH.
HELLLP!

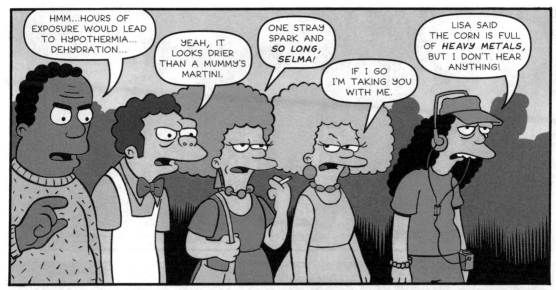

HMM...HOURS OF EXPOSURE WOULD LEAD TO HYPOTHERMIA... DEHYDRATION...

YEAH, IT LOOKS DRIER THAN A MUMMY'S MARTINI.

ONE STRAY SPARK AND *SO LONG, SELMA!*

IF I GO I'M TAKING YOU WITH ME.

LISA SAID THE CORN IS FULL OF *HEAVY METALS,* BUT I DON'T HEAR ANYTHING!

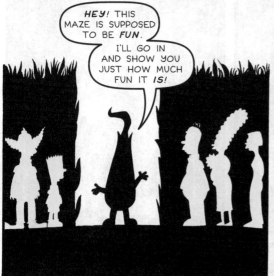

HEY! THIS MAZE IS SUPPOSED TO BE *FUN.*

I'LL GO IN AND SHOW YOU JUST HOW MUCH FUN IT *IS!*

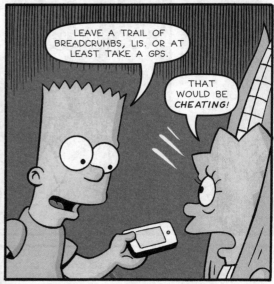

LEAVE A TRAIL OF BREADCRUMBS, LIS. OR AT LEAST TAKE A GPS.

THAT WOULD BE *CHEATING!*

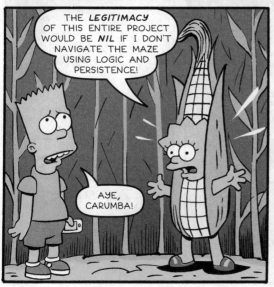

THE *LEGITIMACY* OF THIS ENTIRE PROJECT WOULD BE *NIL* IF I DON'T NAVIGATE THE MAZE USING LOGIC AND PERSISTENCE!

AYE, CARUMBA!

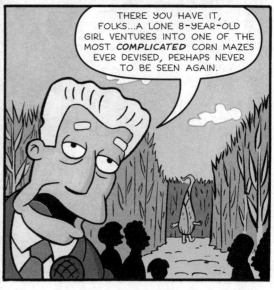

THERE YOU HAVE IT, FOLKS...A LONE 8-YEAR-OLD GIRL VENTURES INTO ONE OF THE MOST *COMPLICATED* CORN MAZES EVER DEVISED, PERHAPS NEVER TO BE SEEN AGAIN.

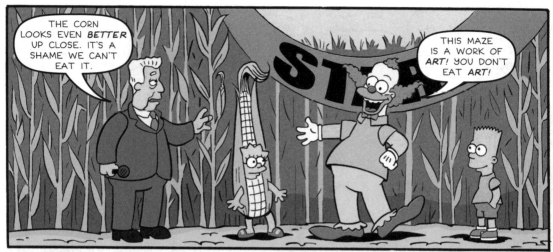

THE CORN LOOKS EVEN *BETTER* UP CLOSE. IT'S A SHAME WE CAN'T EAT IT.

THIS MAZE IS A WORK OF *ART!* YOU DON'T EAT *ART!*

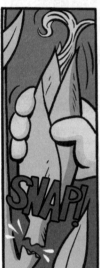

SNAP!

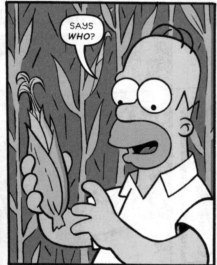

SAYS *WHO?*

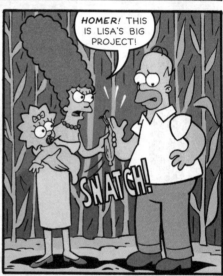

HOMER! THIS IS LISA'S BIG PROJECT!

SNATCH!

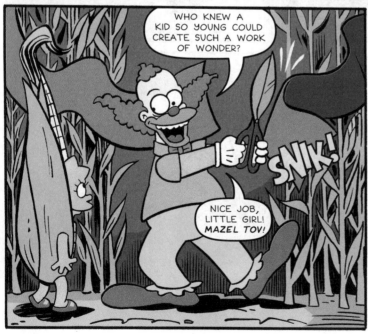

WHO KNEW A KID SO YOUNG COULD CREATE SUCH A WORK OF WONDER?

SNIK!

NICE JOB, LITTLE GIRL! *MAZEL TOV!*

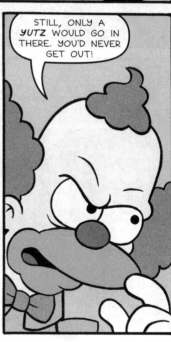

STILL, ONLY A *YUTZ* WOULD GO IN THERE. YOU'D NEVER GET OUT!

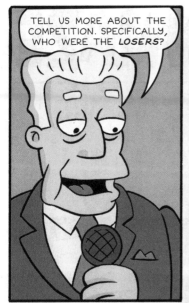

TELL US MORE ABOUT THE COMPETITION. SPECIFICALLY, WHO WERE THE *LOSERS*?

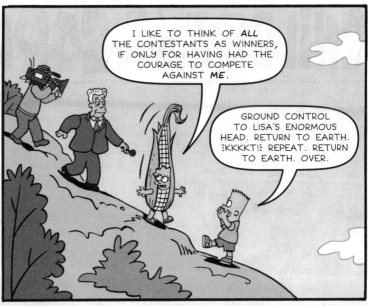

I LIKE TO THINK OF *ALL* THE CONTESTANTS AS WINNERS, IF ONLY FOR HAVING HAD THE COURAGE TO COMPETE AGAINST *ME*.

GROUND CONTROL TO LISA'S ENORMOUS HEAD. RETURN TO EARTH. ≥KKKKT!≤ REPEAT. RETURN TO EARTH. OVER.

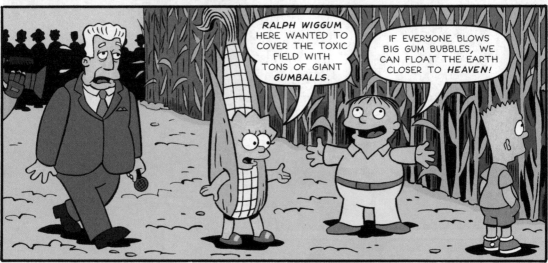

RALPH WIGGUM HERE WANTED TO COVER THE TOXIC FIELD WITH TONS OF GIANT *GUMBALLS*.

IF EVERYONE BLOWS BIG GUM BUBBLES, WE CAN FLOAT THE EARTH CLOSER TO *HEAVEN*!

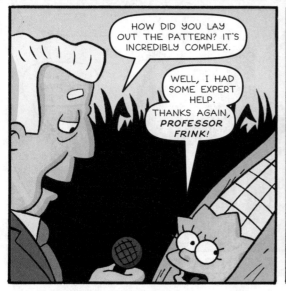

HOW DID YOU LAY OUT THE PATTERN? IT'S INCREDIBLY COMPLEX.

WELL, I HAD SOME EXPERT HELP. THANKS AGAIN, *PROFESSOR FRINK!*

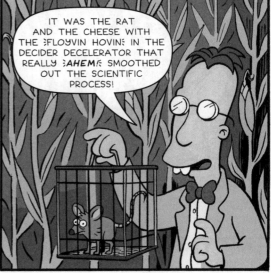

IT WAS THE RAT AND THE CHEESE WITH THE ≥FLOYVIN HOVIN≤ IN THE DECIDER DECELERATOR THAT REALLY ≥AHEM!≤ SMOOTHED OUT THE SCIENTIFIC PROCESS!

CHILDREN OF THE CORN MAZE

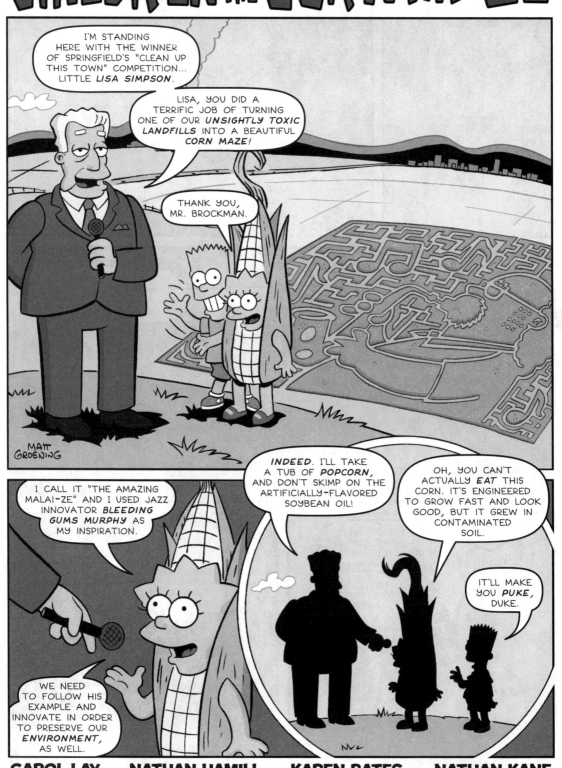

I'M STANDING HERE WITH THE WINNER OF SPRINGFIELD'S "CLEAN UP THIS TOWN" COMPETITION... LITTLE *LISA SIMPSON*.

LISA, YOU DID A TERRIFIC JOB OF TURNING ONE OF OUR *UNSIGHTLY TOXIC LANDFILLS* INTO A BEAUTIFUL *CORN MAZE!*

THANK YOU, MR. BROCKMAN.

I CALL IT "THE AMAZING MALAI-ZE" AND I USED JAZZ INNOVATOR *BLEEDING GUMS MURPHY* AS MY INSPIRATION.

WE NEED TO FOLLOW HIS EXAMPLE AND INNOVATE IN ORDER TO PRESERVE OUR *ENVIRONMENT*, AS WELL.

INDEED. I'LL TAKE A TUB OF *POPCORN*, AND DON'T SKIMP ON THE ARTIFICIALLY-FLAVORED SOYBEAN OIL!

OH, YOU CAN'T ACTUALLY *EAT* THIS CORN. IT'S ENGINEERED TO GROW FAST AND LOOK GOOD, BUT IT GREW IN CONTAMINATED SOIL.

IT'LL MAKE YOU *PUKE*, DUKE.

CAROL LAY
STORY & ART

NATHAN HAMILL
COLORS

KAREN BATES
LETTERS

NATHAN KANE
EDITOR

DIAPERS
DONUTS
DIAPERS

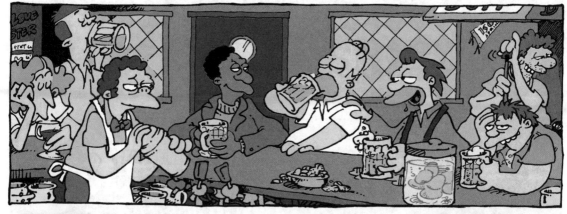

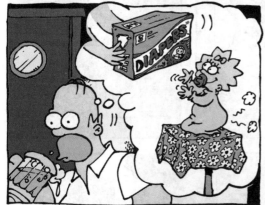

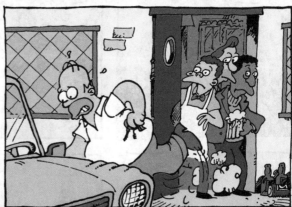

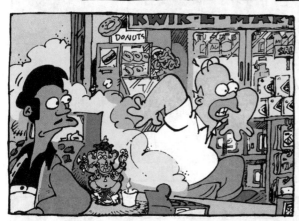

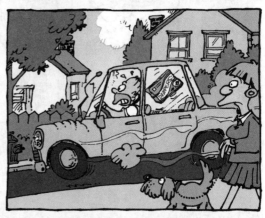

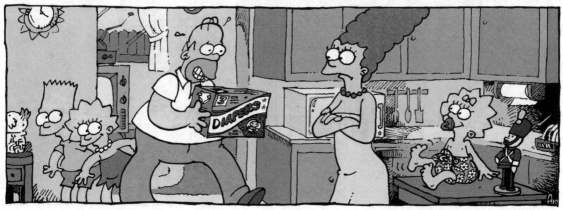

MAGGIE'S CRIB

by ARAGONES

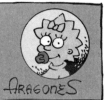

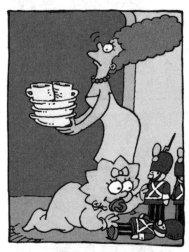
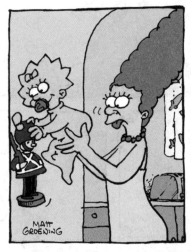
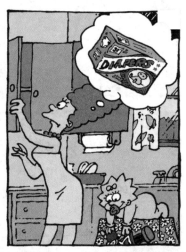

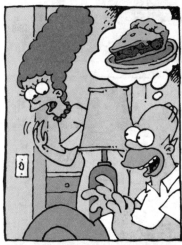
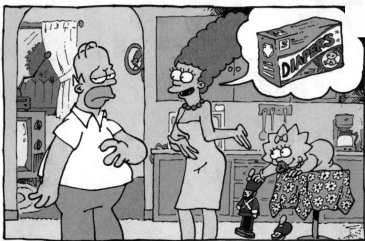

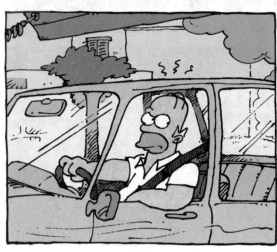
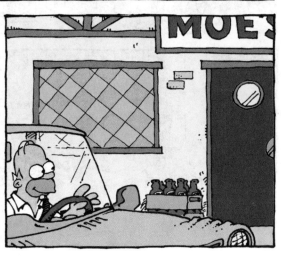

SERGIO ARAGONÉS
STORY & ART

NATHAN HAMILL
COLORS

BILL MORRISON
EDITOR

HERE YOU GO! GRANOLA BARS AND JUICE.
CHOMP!
SLURP!
CHOMP!
PING!
VAMPIRE HIGH!
BYE, MOM!
BYE!
ECISION
ATIGUE
ZOOM
IT'S SO NICE TO SEE SCIENCE CATCHING UP TO WHAT MOTHERS HAVE KNOWN FOR CENTURIES.
ECISION
ATIGUE
END

IS EVERYTHING ALL RIGHT, KIDS?

YEP. LISA GROVELED. I GOT REVENGE. WE'RE GOOD.

JUST FOR THAT, HOW WOULD YOU TWO LIKE TO SEE A *MOVIE*? MY TREAT!

COOL! VAMPIRE HIGH AND *UNIDENTIFIED FLYING SORCERERS* JUST OPENED! *WHICH ONE SHOULD WE SEE?!*

I DON'T *KNOW!* THEY *BOTH* SOUND GREAT!

UFS HAS LOTS OF *FLYING SEQUENCES.*

SO DOES *VAMPIRE HIGH!*

SORCERER HAS *EVIL ELVES.*

DITTO VH!

I'LL BE RIGHT BACK.

WE HAVE TO DECIDE *FAST.* THE SHOWS START *SOON!*

MAYBE WE SHOULD FLIP A *COIN!*

WHAT IF THE COIN IS *WRONG?!*

KIDS, IT'S 4 PM...TIME FOR A LITTLE *SNACK?*

I DON'T HAVE A COIN!

CAN WE FLIP A *DOLLAR BILL?!*

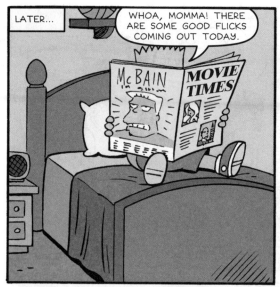

LATER...

WHOA, MOMMA! THERE ARE SOME GOOD FLICKS COMING OUT TODAY.

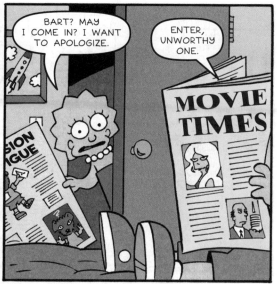

BART? MAY I COME IN? I WANT TO APOLOGIZE.

ENTER, UNWORTHY ONE.

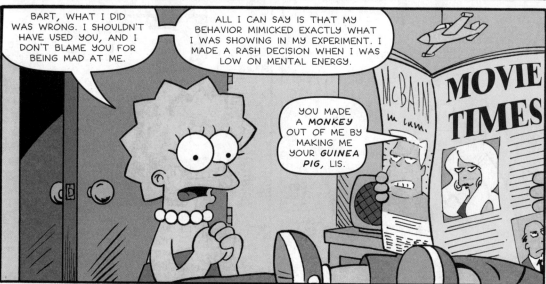

BART, WHAT I DID WAS WRONG. I SHOULDN'T HAVE USED YOU, AND I DON'T BLAME YOU FOR BEING MAD AT ME.

ALL I CAN SAY IS THAT MY BEHAVIOR MIMICKED EXACTLY WHAT I WAS SHOWING IN MY EXPERIMENT. I MADE A RASH DECISION WHEN I WAS LOW ON MENTAL ENERGY.

YOU MADE A *MONKEY* OUT OF ME BY MAKING ME YOUR *GUINEA PIG*, LIS.

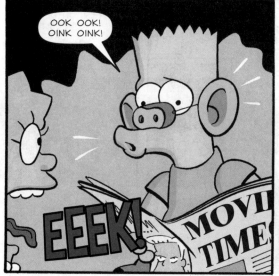

OOK OOK! OINK OINK!

EEEK!

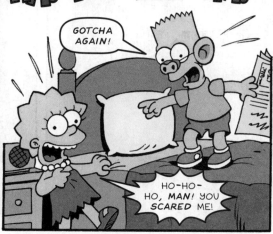

HA! HA! HA! HA!

GOTCHA AGAIN!

HO-HO-HO, MAN! YOU *SCARED* ME!

AT THE SCIENCE FAIR...
HAW HAW! BART THE PIG!
SOO-IE, SOO-IE...PIG PIG PIG!
DECISION FATIGUE
THAT'S NOT A PIG! IT'S A GUINEA PIG! HUGE DIFFERENCE.
GRRR...
I'D GIVE YOU A WEDGIE, BUT I THINK YOU'VE SUFFERED ENOUGH TODAY, MAN.
WORD.
WHY DID YOU DO IT, LIS?
BART, I APOLOGIZE! I HONESTLY DIDN'T THINK ANYONE--
I THOUGHT WE WERE HAVING FUN, BUT YOU WERE JUST USING ME FOR AN EXPERIMENT.
EXIT
OH DEAR. I'M SORRY, BART.

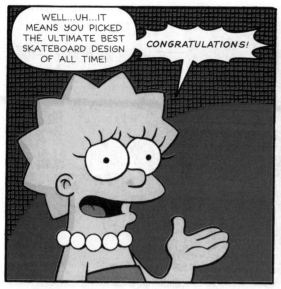

WELL...UH...IT MEANS YOU PICKED THE ULTIMATE BEST SKATEBOARD DESIGN OF ALL TIME!

CONGRATULATIONS!

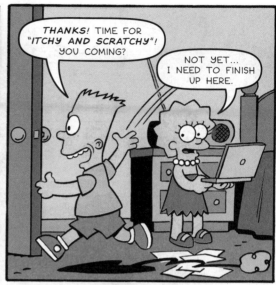

THANKS! TIME FOR *"ITCHY AND SCRATCHY"*! YOU COMING?

NOT YET... I NEED TO FINISH UP HERE.

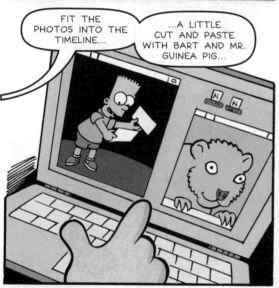

FIT THE PHOTOS INTO THE TIMELINE...

...A LITTLE CUT AND PASTE WITH BART AND MR. GUINEA PIG...

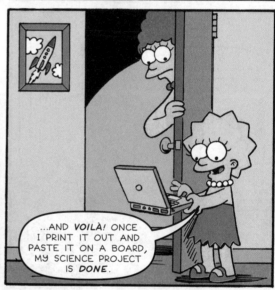

...AND *VOILÀ!* ONCE I PRINT IT OUT AND PASTE IT ON A BOARD, MY SCIENCE PROJECT IS *DONE.*

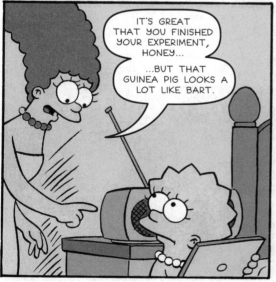

IT'S GREAT THAT YOU FINISHED YOUR EXPERIMENT, HONEY...

...BUT THAT GUINEA PIG LOOKS A LOT LIKE BART.

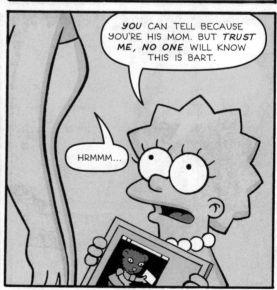

YOU CAN TELL BECAUSE YOU'RE HIS MOM. BUT *TRUST ME, NO ONE* WILL KNOW THIS IS BART.

HRMMM...

LISA...I DON'T FEEL SO GOOD.
MY EYES...
BLEAAGHH!
EEK!
BWA-HA-HA! GOTCHA!
WHEW! FOR A SECOND I THOUGHT YOUR EYES HAD BLISTERED FROM ALL THE WORK WE DID TODAY.
WORK? LOOKING AT ALL THOSE COOL DECKS WAS FUN.
AND I BELIEVE I WAS ABOUT TO PICK THE ULTIMATE RIDE OF THE MILLENNIUM?
CLICK!
DRUM ROLL, PLEASE.
PRUM-RUM-RUM-RUM-RUM-RUM-RUM-RUM...
AND THE WINNER IS...
BOOYA! MELLOW VERT MCGURT!
AND JUST WHAT DOES THAT MEAN, LISA VON PIZZA?
CLICK!

IT'S ALMOST 4 PM, BART...YOU'RE DOING GREAT!
WE'RE DOWN TO THE LAST TWO. A OR B?
HARD TO CARE... SO MANY AWESOME DESIGNS...
YES!
CLICK!
C'MON, BART. WHICH IS BETTER...THE TONYHAWKALOOGIE OR THE MELLOW VERT MCGURT?
I...I JUST DON'T KNOW! I DON'T CARE! I NEED...I NEED...
KNOCK KNOCK, KIDS!
ANYONE CARE FOR AN AFTERNOON SNACK?
SWEET!
THANKS, MOM!
GOOD TIMING!
CHOFF! CHOMP! CHEW!
HIS BEHAVIOR CONFORMED PERFECTLY TO ESTABLISHED LAB FINDINGS.
NOW TO SEE HOW ELEVATED GLUCOSE LEVELS AFFECT HIS ABILITY TO MAKE A LATE-AFTERNOON DECISION.

OKAY, WHICH ONE'S BETTER... A OR B?
A.
WHICH ONE'S BETTER ...A OR B?
B.
BLBB BLUH BLLBB? UBB UH BLUB?
BLUB.
WHICH ONE'S BETTER...A OR B?
A.
WHICH ONE'S BETTER... A OR B?
A.
WHICH ONE'S BETTER ...A OR B?
A.

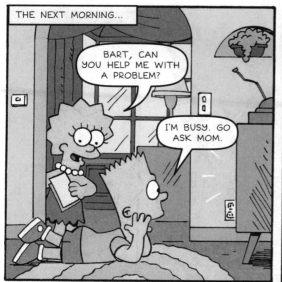

THE NEXT MORNING...

BART, CAN YOU HELP ME WITH A PROBLEM?

I'M BUSY. GO ASK MOM.

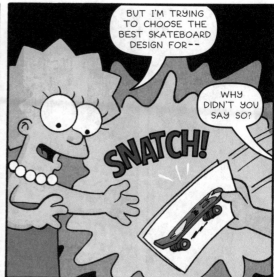

BUT I'M TRYING TO CHOOSE THE BEST SKATEBOARD DESIGN FOR--

WHY DIDN'T YOU SAY SO?

SNATCH!

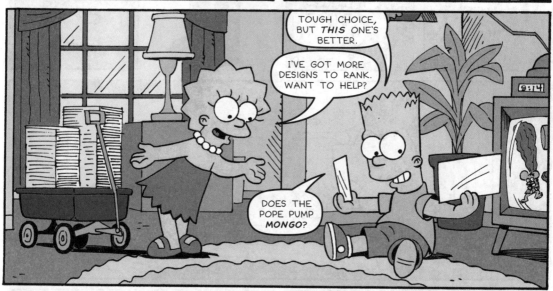

TOUGH CHOICE, BUT *THIS* ONE'S BETTER.

I'VE GOT MORE DESIGNS TO RANK. WANT TO HELP?

DOES THE POPE PUMP *MONGO*?

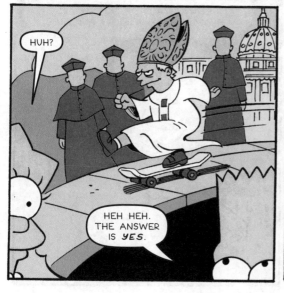

HUH?

HEH HEH. THE ANSWER IS *YES*.

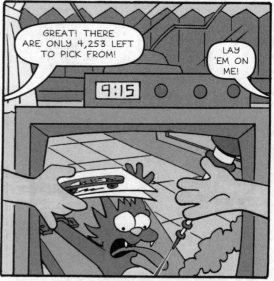

GREAT! THERE ARE ONLY 4,253 LEFT TO PICK FROM!

LAY 'EM ON ME!

9:15

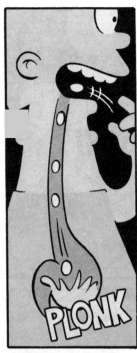

PLONK

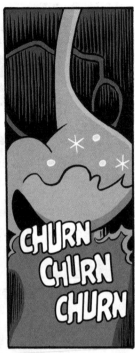

CHURN
CHURN
CHURN

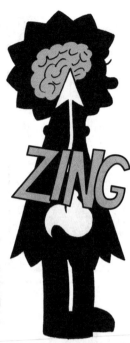

ZING

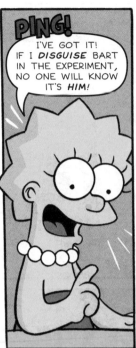

PING!

I'VE GOT IT! IF I *DISGUISE* BART IN THE EXPERIMENT, NO ONE WILL KNOW IT'S *HIM!*

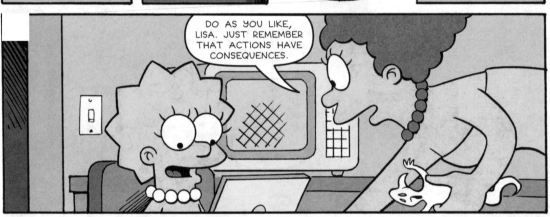

DO AS YOU LIKE, LISA. JUST REMEMBER THAT ACTIONS HAVE CONSEQUENCES.

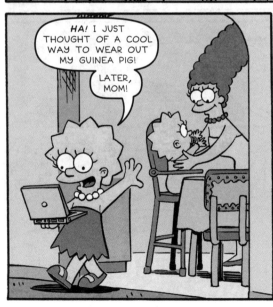

HA! I JUST THOUGHT OF A COOL WAY TO WEAR OUT MY GUINEA PIG!

LATER, MOM!

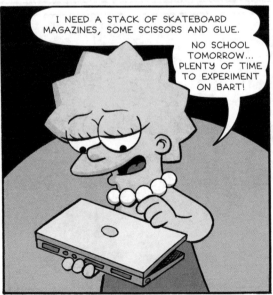

I NEED A STACK OF SKATEBOARD MAGAZINES, SOME SCISSORS AND GLUE.

NO SCHOOL TOMORROW... PLENTY OF TIME TO EXPERIMENT ON BART!

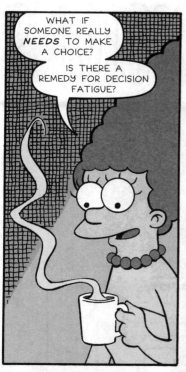

WHAT IF SOMEONE REALLY *NEEDS* TO MAKE A CHOICE?

IS THERE A REMEDY FOR DECISION FATIGUE?

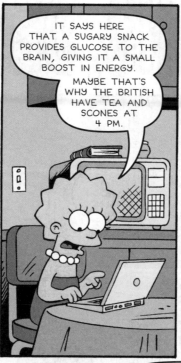

IT SAYS HERE THAT A SUGARY SNACK PROVIDES GLUCOSE TO THE BRAIN, GIVING IT A SMALL BOOST IN ENERGY.

MAYBE THAT'S WHY THE BRITISH HAVE TEA AND SCONES AT 4 PM.

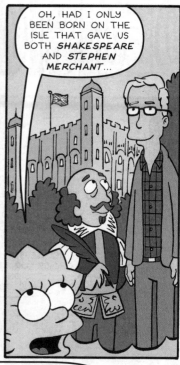

OH, HAD I ONLY BEEN BORN ON THE ISLE THAT GAVE US BOTH *SHAKESPEARE* AND *STEPHEN MERCHANT*...

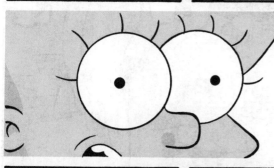

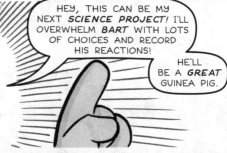

HEY, THIS CAN BE MY NEXT *SCIENCE PROJECT!* I'LL OVERWHELM *BART* WITH LOTS OF CHOICES AND RECORD HIS REACTIONS!

HE'LL BE A *GREAT* GUINEA PIG.

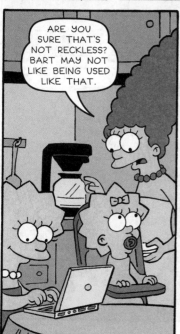

ARE YOU SURE THAT'S NOT RECKLESS? BART MAY NOT LIKE BEING USED LIKE THAT.

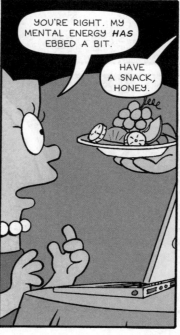

YOU'RE RIGHT. MY MENTAL ENERGY *HAS* EBBED A BIT.

HAVE A SNACK, HONEY.

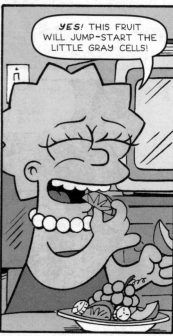

YES! THIS FRUIT WILL JUMP-START THE LITTLE GRAY CELLS!

DECISIONS, DECISIONS

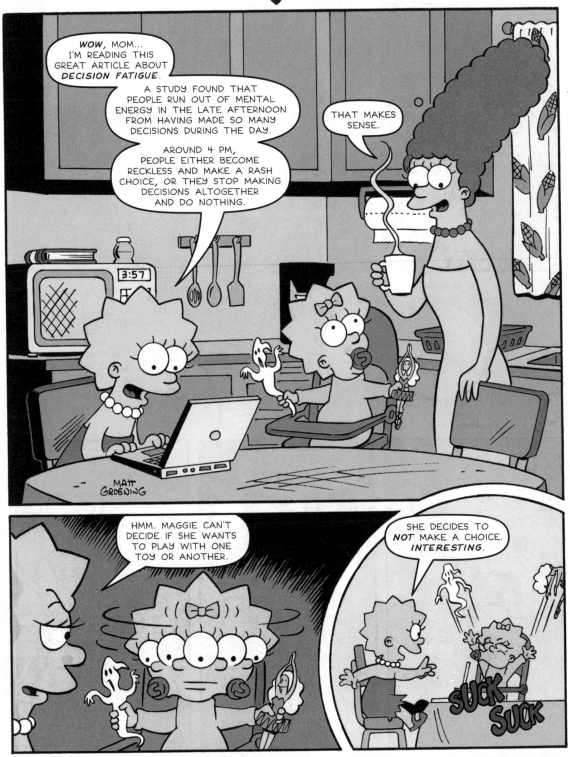

WOW, MOM... I'M READING THIS GREAT ARTICLE ABOUT *DECISION FATIGUE.*

A STUDY FOUND THAT PEOPLE RUN OUT OF MENTAL ENERGY IN THE LATE AFTERNOON FROM HAVING MADE SO MANY DECISIONS DURING THE DAY.

AROUND 4 PM, PEOPLE EITHER BECOME RECKLESS AND MAKE A RASH CHOICE, OR THEY STOP MAKING DECISIONS ALTOGETHER AND DO NOTHING.

THAT MAKES SENSE.

HMM. MAGGIE CAN'T DECIDE IF SHE WANTS TO PLAY WITH ONE TOY OR ANOTHER.

SHE DECIDES TO *NOT* MAKE A CHOICE. *INTERESTING.*

SUCK SUCK

CAROL LAY
STORY & ART

NATHAN HAMILL
COLORS

KAREN BATES
LETTERS

NATHAN KANE
EDITOR

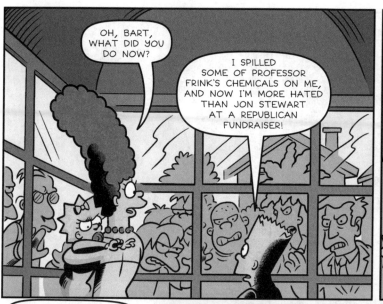

OH, BART, WHAT DID YOU DO NOW?

I SPILLED SOME OF PROFESSOR FRINK'S CHEMICALS ON ME, AND NOW I'M MORE HATED THAN JON STEWART AT A REPUBLICAN FUNDRAISER!

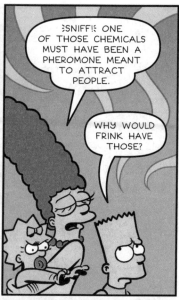

:SNIFF!: ONE OF THOSE CHEMICALS MUST HAVE BEEN A PHEROMONE MEANT TO ATTRACT PEOPLE.

WHY WOULD FRINK HAVE THOSE?

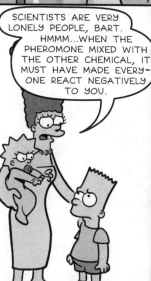

SCIENTISTS ARE VERY LONELY PEOPLE, BART. HMMM...WHEN THE PHEROMONE MIXED WITH THE OTHER CHEMICAL, IT MUST HAVE MADE EVERYONE REACT NEGATIVELY TO YOU.

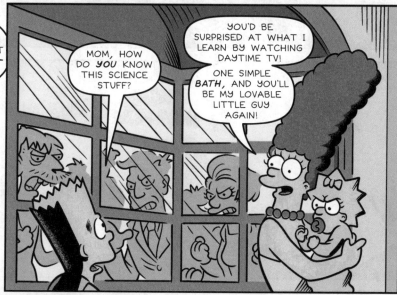

MOM, HOW DO *YOU* KNOW THIS SCIENCE STUFF?

YOU'D BE SURPRISED AT WHAT I LEARN BY WATCHING DAYTIME TV!

ONE SIMPLE *BATH*, AND YOU'LL BE MY LOVABLE LITTLE GUY AGAIN!

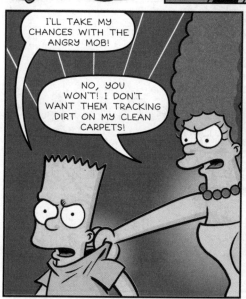

I'LL TAKE MY CHANCES WITH THE ANGRY MOB!

NO, YOU WON'T! I DON'T WANT THEM TRACKING DIRT ON MY CLEAN CARPETS!

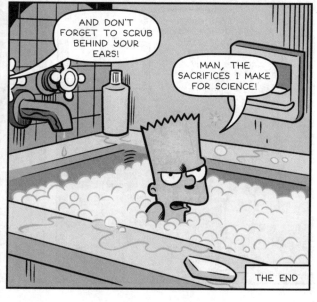

AND DON'T FORGET TO SCRUB BEHIND YOUR EARS!

MAN, THE SACRIFICES I MAKE FOR SCIENCE!

THE END

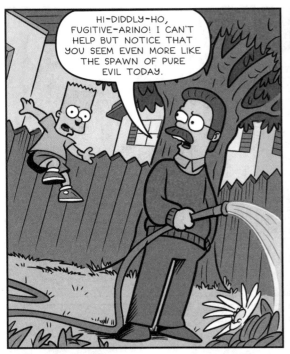

HI-DIDDLY-HO, FUGITIVE-ARINO! I CAN'T HELP BUT NOTICE THAT YOU SEEM EVEN MORE LIKE THE SPAWN OF PURE EVIL TODAY.

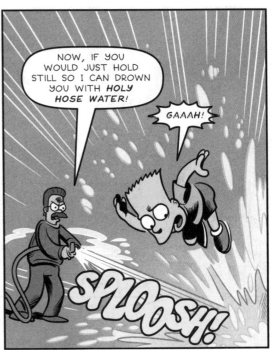

NOW, IF YOU WOULD JUST HOLD STILL SO I CAN DROWN YOU WITH *HOLY HOSE WATER*!

GAAAH!

SPLOOSH!

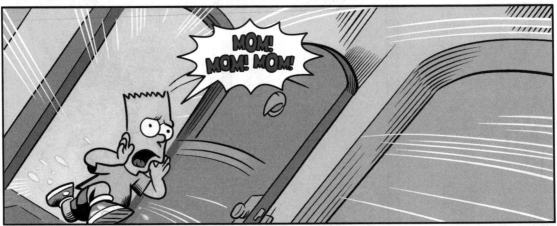

MOM! MOM! MOM!

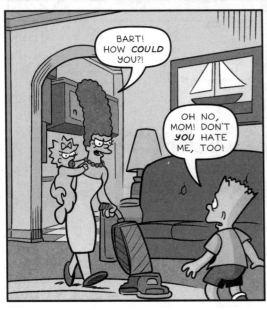

BART! HOW *COULD* YOU?!

OH NO, MOM! DON'T *YOU* HATE ME, TOO!

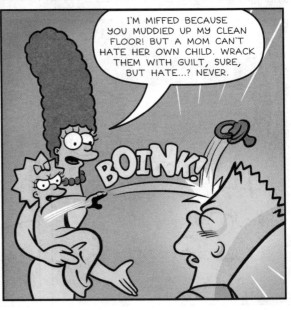

I'M MIFFED BECAUSE YOU MUDDIED UP MY CLEAN FLOOR! BUT A MOM CAN'T HATE HER OWN CHILD. WRACK THEM WITH GUILT, SURE, BUT HATE...? NEVER.

BOINK!

YOU RUINED MY FIGURE!
YOU CONVINCED ME TO VOTE FOR RON PAUL!
I SELL YOUR FATHER BOOZE EVERY NIGHT. DO YOU EVER CALL TO THANK ME? NO!
WASHROOMS
WHY, YOU LITTLE--!
LET ME TAKE A WHACK AT THAT LITTLE MOLE!
SMASH!
OWWW! MOE!
SORRY, HOMER. I NEVER WAS MUCH GOOD AT SPORTS...OR WITH WORDS...OR WITH WOMEN.
MANY ANGRY PEOPLE LATER...
HE HAD THE AUDACITY TO SAY MY UNCANNY X-MEN #137 IS MERELY IN GOOD CONDITION, NOT GOOD PLUS!
MY HATRED OF HIM IS MAKING ME MISS WORK...WHICH MAKES ME HATE HIM EVEN MORE!
HE TOLD DISCO STU THAT KOOL AND THE GANG WERE NEITHER COOL NOR A GANG!

I ALWAYS LOOK FORWARD TO OUR 1:20 DONUT BREAK.
TECHNICALLY, CHIEF, THESE ARE *CRULLERS*.
CHIEF WIGGUM! EVERYBODY AT THE SCHOOL WANTS TO KILL ME!
GEEZ, KID! WHY'D YOU INTERRUPT OUR BREAK? WE'RE ONLY ALLOTTED *SIX* PER DAY!
LET ME TASE HIM, CHIEF.
LOU, FOR THE LAST TIME...WITH THE *THREE-STRIKES LAW,* WE'RE SUPPOSED TO STRIKE THEM THREE TIMES, *THEN* TASE THEM.
UH, CHIEF? DO I HAVE TO EXPLAIN THIS TO YOU AGAIN?
WHY MUST WE ALWAYS ARGUE LIKE THIS BEFORE AN ARREST? YOU AND YOUR "POLICE BRUTALITY" NONSENSE.
HE'S GETTING AWAY!
EVERYBODY'S GONE CRAZY! I NEED TO FIND HOMER! AFTER ALL, WHO KNOWS *CRAZY* BETTER THAN *HIM?*
HMMM...HE SHOULD BE AT WORK NOW, SO THAT MEANS...
HOMER! I NEED FATHERLY PROTECTION!

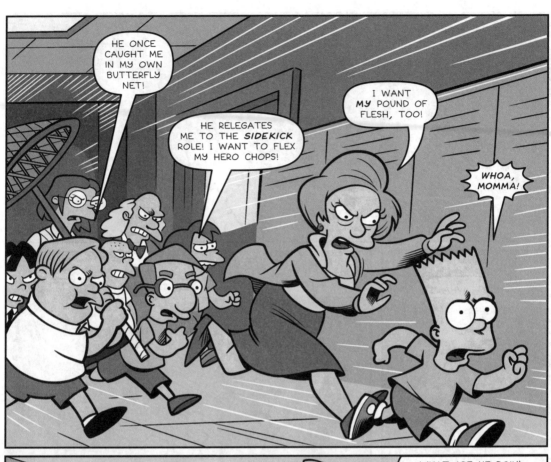

HE ONCE CAUGHT ME IN MY OWN BUTTERFLY NET!

HE RELEGATES ME TO THE *SIDEKICK* ROLE! I WANT TO FLEX MY HERO CHOPS!

I WANT *MY* POUND OF FLESH, TOO!

WHOA, MOMMA!

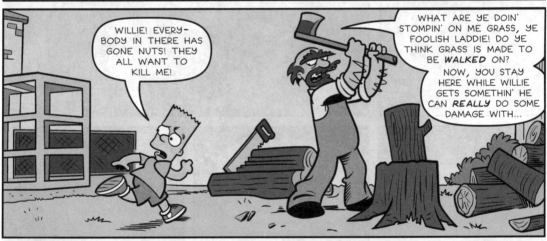

WILLIE! EVERYBODY IN THERE HAS GONE NUTS! THEY ALL WANT TO KILL ME!

WHAT ARE YE DOIN' STOMPIN' ON ME GRASS, YE FOOLISH LADDIE! DO YE THINK GRASS IS MADE TO BE *WALKED* ON?

NOW, YOU STAY HERE WHILE WILLIE GETS SOMETHIN' HE CAN *REALLY* DO SOME DAMAGE WITH...

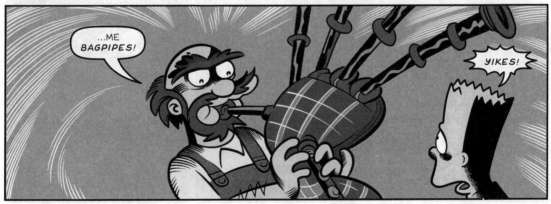

...ME BAGPIPES!

YIKES!

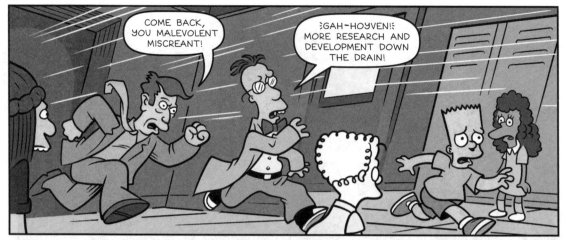

COME BACK, YOU MALEVOLENT MISCREANT!

⁜GAH-HOYVEN!⁜ MORE RESEARCH AND DEVELOPMENT DOWN THE DRAIN!

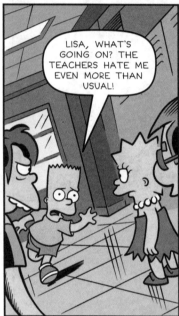

LISA, WHAT'S GOING ON? THE TEACHERS HATE ME EVEN MORE THAN USUAL!

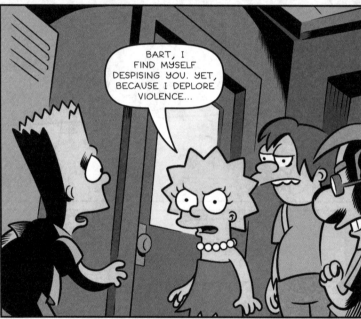

BART, I FIND MYSELF DESPISING YOU. YET, BECAUSE I DEPLORE VIOLENCE...

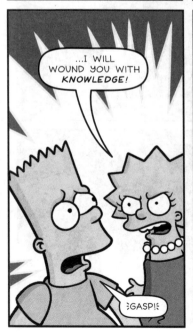

...I WILL WOUND YOU WITH *KNOWLEDGE!*

⁜GASP!⁜

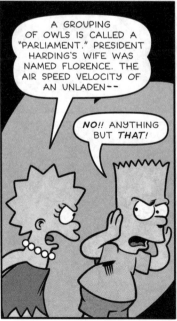

A GROUPING OF OWLS IS CALLED A "PARLIAMENT." PRESIDENT HARDING'S WIFE WAS NAMED FLORENCE. THE AIR SPEED VELOCITY OF AN UNLADEN--

NO!! ANYTHING BUT *THAT!*

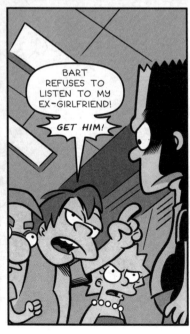

BART REFUSES TO LISTEN TO MY EX-GIRLFRIEND! *GET HIM!*

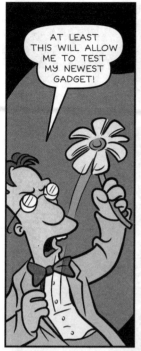

AT LEAST THIS WILL ALLOW ME TO TEST MY NEWEST GADGET!

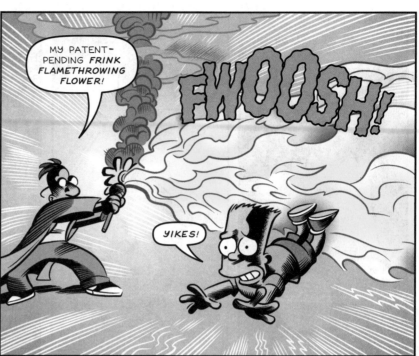

MY PATENT-PENDING *FRINK FLAMETHROWING FLOWER!*

FWOOSH!

YIKES!

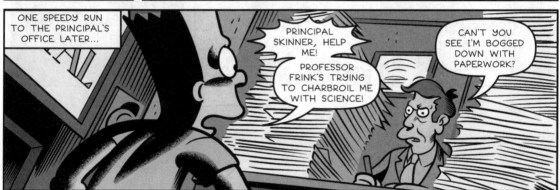

ONE SPEEDY RUN TO THE PRINCIPAL'S OFFICE LATER...

PRINCIPAL SKINNER, HELP ME!

PROFESSOR FRINK'S TRYING TO CHARBROIL ME WITH SCIENCE!

CAN'T YOU SEE I'M BOGGED DOWN WITH PAPERWORK?

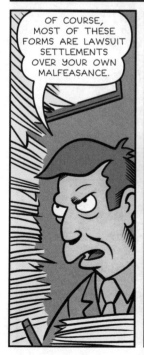

OF COURSE, MOST OF THESE FORMS ARE LAWSUIT SETTLEMENTS OVER YOUR OWN MALFEASANCE.

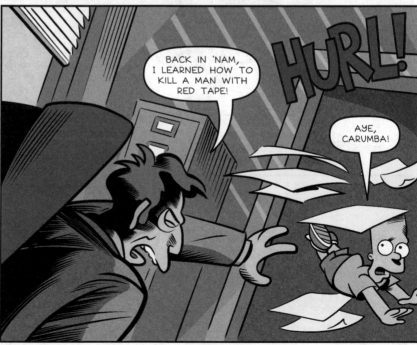

BACK IN 'NAM, I LEARNED HOW TO KILL A MAN WITH RED TAPE!

HURL!

AYE, CARUMBA!

WHY, HE'D ENTERTAIN THE CROWD!
WOW, JUGGLING REALLY IS AS HARD AS IT LOOKS.
CRASH!
SPLOTCH!
UH-OH!
EGADS! WHAT IN THE NAME OF DYNAMIC VISCOSITY HAS TRANSPIRED?
SORRY, DOC. AT LEAST YOU KNOW ***GRAVITY*** IS STILL WORKING.
GIANT FEELINGS OF ⁝GLAVIN⁝ RISING INSIDE ME LIKE...OPPENHEIMER BECOMING THE ***DESTROYER OF WORLDS!***

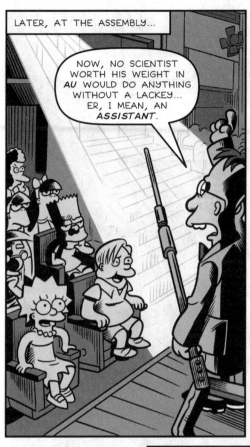

LATER, AT THE ASSEMBLY...

NOW, NO SCIENTIST WORTH HIS WEIGHT IN *AU* WOULD DO ANYTHING WITHOUT A LACKEY... ER, I MEAN, AN *ASSISTANT*.

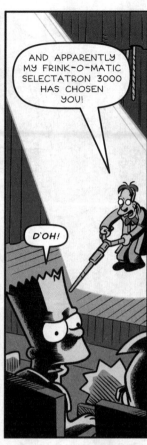

AND APPARENTLY MY FRINK-O-MATIC SELECTATRON 3000 HAS CHOSEN *YOU!*

D'OH!

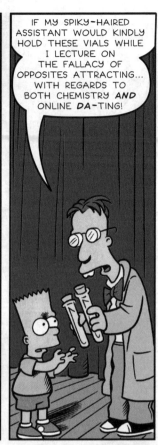

IF MY SPIKY-HAIRED ASSISTANT WOULD KINDLY HOLD THESE VIALS WHILE I LECTURE ON THE FALLACY OF OPPOSITES ATTRACTING... WITH REGARDS TO BOTH CHEMISTRY *AND* ONLINE *DA*-TING!

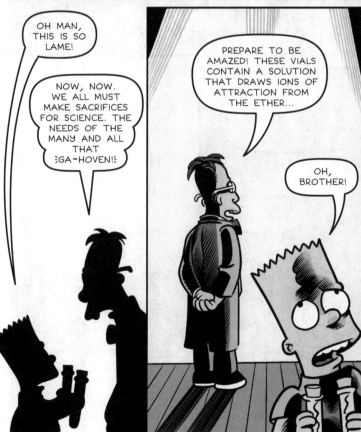

OH MAN, THIS IS SO LAME!

NOW, NOW. WE ALL MUST MAKE SACRIFICES FOR SCIENCE. THE NEEDS OF THE MANY AND ALL THAT *:GA-HOVEN!:*

PREPARE TO BE AMAZED! THESE VIALS CONTAIN A SOLUTION THAT DRAWS IONS OF ATTRACTION FROM THE ETHER...

OH, BROTHER!

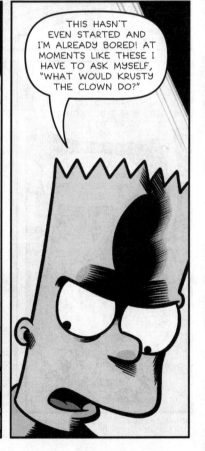

THIS HASN'T EVEN STARTED AND I'M ALREADY BORED! AT MOMENTS LIKE THESE I HAVE TO ASK MYSELF, "WHAT WOULD KRUSTY THE CLOWN DO?"

EVERYBODY REALLY HATES BART

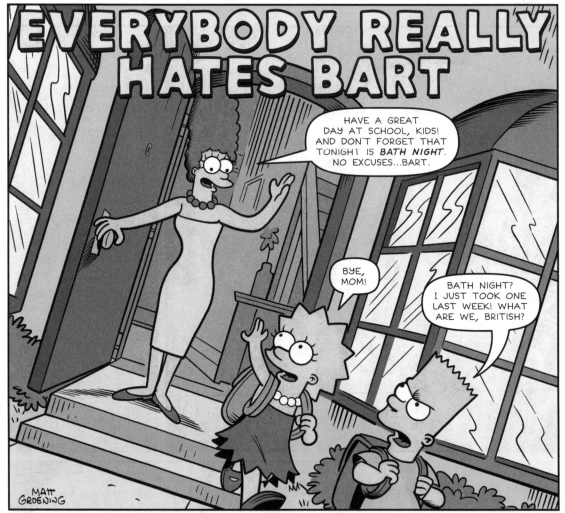

HAVE A GREAT DAY AT SCHOOL, KIDS! AND DON'T FORGET THAT TONIGHT IS *BATH NIGHT*. NO EXCUSES...BART.

BYE, MOM!

BATH NIGHT? I JUST TOOK ONE LAST WEEK! WHAT ARE WE, BRITISH?

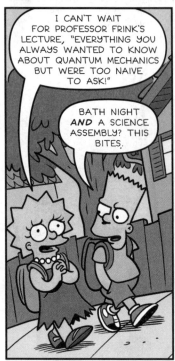

I CAN'T WAIT FOR PROFESSOR FRINK'S LECTURE, "EVERYTHING YOU ALWAYS WANTED TO KNOW ABOUT QUANTUM MECHANICS BUT WERE TOO NAIVE TO ASK!"

BATH NIGHT *AND* A SCIENCE ASSEMBLY? THIS BITES.

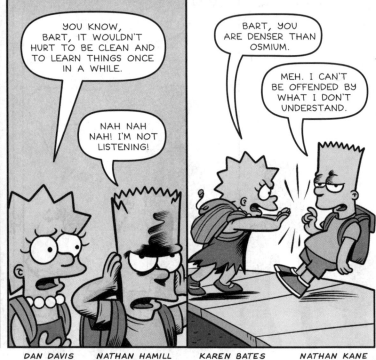

YOU KNOW, BART, IT WOULDN'T HURT TO BE CLEAN AND TO LEARN THINGS ONCE IN A WHILE.

NAH NAH NAH! I'M NOT LISTENING!

BART, YOU ARE DENSER THAN OSMIUM.

MEH. I CAN'T BE OFFENDED BY WHAT I DON'T UNDERSTAND.

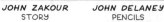

JOHN ZAKOUR STORY   **JOHN DELANEY** PENCILS   **DAN DAVIS** INKS   **NATHAN HAMILL** COLORS   **KAREN BATES** LETTERS   **NATHAN KANE** EDITOR